Pictorial History of Princeton

Pictorial History of
Princeton

EDITED BY WHEATON J. LANE

PRINCETON, NEW JERSEY

PRINCETON UNIVERSITY PRESS

1947

Copyright 1947 by Princeton University Press
London: Geoffrey Cumberlege, Oxford University Press

Printed in the United States of America by Meriden
Gravure Company at Meriden, Connecticut

Preface and Acknowledgment

This publication is the result of the joint suggestion of the Office of Public Relations of Princeton University and the Princeton University Press. The wealth of illustrative material that has accumulated during the two hundred years of Princeton's history makes it seem logical to produce at this time a pictorial history of Princeton as college and university.

The very abundance of pictures, portraits, manuscripts, prints, and other graphic material has proved a source of embarrassment. Certain subjects, herein suggested by a picture or two, would have been greatly expanded had space permitted. Among undergraduate activities, for example, the Triangle Club, sports, or football alone, would provide enough material for a book as large as this. The compiler—not author, since text has been kept at a minimum—thus presents his apology to those alumni and faculty who may wonder why some picture especially significant to them has been omitted.

Mr. Edmund S. DeLong and Mr. Datus C. Smith, Jr., have been the guiding spirits in the compilation of this book; and the former has written most of the captions relating to living persons. Mr. Frederick S. Osborne and Mr. Dan D. Coyle of the Office of Public Relations, and Mr. P. J. Conkwright and Mrs. Helen Van Zandt of the University Press have also suggested valuable ideas, and the last two have labored over the problem of format and layout. To all these I am especially grateful.

Certain information regarding Princeton's history has been supplied by Thomas J. Wertenbaker, Edwards Professor of American History, who kindly loaned me his manuscript history of Princeton; by Mr. Neilson Poe, at once the Nestor and Ajax of Princeton athletics; and by Mr. Philip A. Rollins, Professor Thomas M. Parrott, Mr. Andrew C. Imbrie, Professor J. Duncan Spaeth, Professor William S. Myers, Professor Donald D. Egbert, Professor Henry L. Savage, and Professor Robert McN. McElroy. Mr. Carl Zigrosser of the Philadelphia Museum of Art kindly made researches concerning the origin of the seal of the College of New Jersey.

Pictures have been loaned or given to me by a host of alumni, faculty, friends, and offices of the University. The list is too long for inclusion here, but I must express my obligation to Mr. Albridge C. Smith, Mrs. Robert M. Scoon, Professor William K. Prentice, Mr. John Jay Johns, Mr. Robert V. C. Whitehead, Jr., Mrs. G. Howard Bright, Mrs. T. Hart Anderson, and Mr. Arthur M. Conger. Mr. Samuel Chamberlain and the Princeton Print Club graciously allowed me to reproduce as frontispiece Mr. Chamberlain's recent drypoint of Nassau Hall. Mr. Archibald G. Murray kindly permitted me to reproduce an illustration from his *Sketches of the Sesquicentennial*.

Many of the portraits reproduced herein are owned by art galleries, historical societies, and by universities other than Princeton. Proper acknowledgment will be found in the caption accompanying each. In certain cases it has been found necessary to crop the portrait. Where outside portraits are used, they are usually superior to those owned by the University.

In the compiling of pictures I have been greatly aided by Miss Julie Hudson and Miss Lillian Blease of the Treasure Room of the University Library. Doubtless I have annoyed them excessively, but they have long and cheerfully delved into collections and files upon my mere suggestion.

Practically all the modern photographs which do not bear a credit line have been taken by the Princeton Photo Service. Their number is so great that I wish to acknowledge their reproduction here, as well as the efficient work of the staff undergraduates, especially that of Mr. Robert R. Lane. A few photographs, taken in the 1930's, are by Mr. Frank Kane who, having left the field of photography, states that he has no interest in a credit line. Other commercial photographers receive credit lines, but mention might well be made here of Mr. Alan W. Richards, who took the aerial photographs.

Where recognition of individuals in pictures depends upon memory, error invariably creeps in. I shall be grateful for having my attention called to any errors in caption or text.

WHEATON J. LANE

Table of Contents

Preface and Acknowledgment	v
THE EARLY PERIOD 1746-1795	1
The Presidents	2
Landmarks and Memorabilia	5
Alumni of the Early Period	14
THE MIDDLE PERIOD 1795-1888	19
The Presidents	20
Faculty Leaders	23
Buildings and Views	29
Alumni of the Middle Period	51
THE RECENT PERIOD 1888-1947	57
The Presidents	58
Administration and Faculty	60
Buildings and Views	77
PRINCETON IN WAR	105
UNDERGRADUATE LIFE	119
Curricular	119
Customs and Traditions	128
Campus Activities	142
Social Life	152
Approaching the End	156
Athletics	158
ALUMNI REUNIONS	176
PRINCETON'S ANNIVERSARIES	181
Index	199

NASSAU HALL
From a recent drypoint by Samuel Chamberlain.

The Early Period 1746-1795

THE history of Princeton falls into three natural divisions. The early or what might justifiably be called the heroic period of the College of New Jersey comprises its founding, its remarkable development under Witherspoon when it was literally "a school of statesmen," and its tribulations during the American Revolution. The accession of Samuel Stanhope Smith to the presidency in 1795 marked the beginning of a century of history in which Princeton, after reaching a point at which its friends despaired of its future, slowly climbed until the great administration of James McCosh transformed it in all but name to a university. After the accession of Francis L. Patton in 1888, the old College of New Jersey became Princeton University at the time of the sesquicentennial anniversary. The past fifty years comprise a period of almost continuous growth, interrupted only by war.

It has been truly said that education in colonial America was the child of religion. Princeton's predecessors, Harvard, William and Mary, and Yale, were all established by religious denominations. The College of New Jersey came into being as the result of the Great Awakening, that famous religious revival of the second quarter of the eighteenth century. Emphasizing the need of personal religious experience, revivalists like the Tennents and George Whitefield attracted multitudes of adherents. In the Presbyterian Church, these became known as New Lights as opposed to the Old Sides who preferred more conservative methods. It was this new group which was instrumental in the founding of Princeton.

"The plan and foundation" was first "concocted" by four ministers and three laymen. Jonathan Dickinson of Elizabeth, Aaron Burr of Newark, John Pierson of Woodbridge, and Ebenezer Pemberton of New York were all in full sympathy with the New Lights, as were the laymen, William Smith, Peter Van Brugh Livingston, and William Peartree Smith, all of New York. Six of these were graduates of Yale and one of Harvard, but they were agreed that the New England colleges were too conservative. On October 22, 1746, John Hamilton, Acting Governor of New Jersey, affixed his signature to a charter empowering the seven to act as trustees of the new College of New Jersey.

In May of 1747 the first handful of students met in the parsonage of Jonathan Dickinson at Elizabeth. The College was now an actuality, possessing charter, trustees, faculty, and students. Dickinson was elected President. Later that year, the trustees were enlarged by the addition of several men formerly associated with the Log College. This school, founded twenty years before by the elder William Tennent, had been a stronghold of New Light influence; but it is inaccurate to state that the College of New Jersey grew out of the Neshaminy school, as several historians have claimed.

On the death of Dickinson the College was moved to Newark where Aaron Burr gathered the students into his household. In 1748 Governor Belcher granted the College its second charter, ending the attacks of those who claimed that the first was illegal because Hamilton had been only Acting Governor. Belcher later became the patron of the College, giving it his large library. He also broadened the board of trustees by including laymen from New Jersey and Pennsylvania.

With the successful raising of funds, the trustees decided upon a permanent location in Princeton. A mere stage stop for travelers, this town was chosen because of the inducements it offered and because of its central location. The cornerstone of Nassau Hall was put in place in September 1754, and two years later Burr and the students made the trip from Newark to Princeton.

Nassau Hall, as the College now came to be known, was fortunate in having able Presidents; but unfortunate in that the early ones had short careers. Dickinson, Burr, Edwards, Davies, and Finley all had short administrations; and all were overworked.

The arrival of John Witherspoon from Scotland in 1768 marked the beginning of one of the most illustrious administrations in Princeton's history. Endowment funds were secured, the faculty was enlarged, and scientific apparatus, including the famous Rittenhouse orrery, was acquired. Although a recent arrival from Britain, Witherspoon became an ardent champion of American rights and the College attracted the sons of families which were of Whig persuasion. His own political career, culminating in his plea for Independence and his signature to the Declaration, endeared him to all American patriots.

The College of New Jersey suffered severely in the Revolution. Nassau Hall was pillaged by troops of both sides and it came under the fire of Washington's artillery in the Battle of Princeton. Currency inflation added greatly to financial troubles. But slowly the battered walls of Nassau Hall were restored.

The great event of Witherspoon's administration occurred when Congress came to sit in Nassau Hall during the summer and fall of 1783. Here Congress received General Washington in August, and tendered him the thanks of the country for his wartime services. In the commencement of that fall there were present seven signers of the Declaration and eleven future signers of the Constitution, many of them graduates of the "school of statesmen." William Peartree Smith, the last active trustee of the original seven, must have thought that the College had truly flourished under the favor of God.

The Presidents

JONATHAN DICKINSON 1747

AARON BURR 1748-1757

JONATHAN DICKINSON, elected in 1747 as the first President of the College of New Jersey, was the obvious and inevitable choice of the trustees. "The eminently learned, faithful, and pious" minister of the Presbyterian Church at Elizabeth, a distinguished writer and theologian, a graduate of Yale in 1706, was one of seven men who first "concocted the plan and foundation" of the College.

For several years before 1747 he had conducted a school at his parsonage, and his scholars undoubtedly formed the nucleus of the small group of undergraduates which first met in that year. Assisted by one tutor, President Dickinson gave instruction that was necessarily informal and intimate, perhaps not unlike that of a modern preceptorial.

The infant College received a severe blow when he died, only four and a half months after the opening. Yet he had founded so well that, despite universal sorrow, there was no despair of the future of the institution.

(This reproduction is from the portrait of Dickinson, painted by Edward L. Mooney, which hangs in the Faculty Room in Nassau Hall.)

AARON BURR, the second President, took over the care of the infant College upon the death of Dickinson. A graduate of Yale in 1735, he was the youngest President to hold office. The College was transferred to Newark, where Burr was pastor of the Old First Church.

To President Burr belongs the honor of the organization of the curriculum of the College, together with its ceremonies, and its discipline. The first commencement was held in the church in November 1748, and the ceremonies were elaborate. They comprised an academic procession to the church, and a formal reading of the new charter. Later Burr delivered, as his inaugural address, a Latin oration on the value of liberal learning. Then followed the disputations of the six graduating students, likewise in Latin. Degrees were then bestowed, while Governor Belcher received the degree of Master, *honoris causa*. A reporter recorded that everyone was quite satisfied, "even the unlearned being pleased with the external solemnity and decorum."

In the fall of 1756 President Burr brought the College to Princeton, where Nassau Hall was approaching completion. In his task of administration he was greatly aided by his wife Esther, the daughter of Jonathan Edwards. After a year in Princeton he died from overwork.

(From a copy by Edward L. Mooney in the Faculty Room, which is from a portrait possibly by Stuart.)

JONATHAN EDWARDS, one of the greatest intellects America has produced, was President only thirty-four days. The father-in-law of Aaron Burr, he was called to Princeton from Stockbridge, Massachusetts, where he was pastor and missionary to the Indians.

A graduate of Yale in the class of 1720—he was just seventeen at the time—he entered the ministry and was long settled at the Congregational Church in Northampton. He was an ardent evangelist, a friend of George Whitefield, and a leader in the Great Awakening; but his famous sermon, "Sinners in the Hands of an Angry God," was not typical. It was as metaphysician that Edwards won his greatest fame; his treatise "On the Freedom of the Will" standing as one of the outstanding classics of philosophical thought.

Edwards' coming to Princeton was tragic. Smallpox was then prevalent and it was thought advisable to submit the new President to inoculation. Dr. William Shippen, co-architect of Nassau Hall, came from Philadelphia for the purpose. Edwards died of the disease he was trying to avoid. The greatest American theologian of the eighteenth century fell a victim to the new science.

(From a portrait of Edwards by Joseph Badger, reproduced by courtesy of the Yale University Art Gallery.)

JONATHAN EDWARDS 1758

SAMUEL DAVIES, fourth President, was reluctant to accept the call to Princeton, despite his great services to the College in its earliest days. In 1753, with Gilbert Tennent, he had gone to England to raise funds for the new institution, and their success had made possible the construction of Nassau Hall and the President's House.

He received his education at Samuel Blair's famous academy at Fagg's Manor, Pennsylvania, and thus fell heir to the influence of the Log College. He was early sent as an evangelist to Virginia, where dissenters were regarded with hostility. He achieved fame by personally carrying to the King in Council the question as to whether the Act of Toleration extended to the colony, and won his case.

Despite Davies' modesty and sincere doubts as to his fitness for the position, he made an excellent President. Scholarly, very eloquent in the pulpit, and receptive to new trends in education, he was equally liked by trustees and students. Like Burr, he drove himself to overwork; and tuberculosis took his life in 1761. His death, it is recorded, dismayed the College "and spread a gloom all over the country."

(From the portrait by James Massalon that hangs in the Faculty Room.)

SAMUEL DAVIES 1759-1761

SAMUEL FINLEY 1761-1766

SAMUEL FINLEY was unanimously elected President upon the death of Samuel Davies. Finley had been born in Ireland, and as a youth had come to Philadelphia determined to enter the ministry. It is amusing to recall that in his early career he accepted an invitation to preach before the "Second Society" at New Haven; as this organization was not recognized by the authorities, he was arrested and sentenced to be deported from the colony as an interloper and vagrant.

In 1744 Finley settled as a pastor at Nottingham on the Pennsylvania-Maryland border, where he conducted an academy. He became a trustee of the College of New Jersey under the original charter of 1746, and reentered the board in 1751; ten years later he was the obvious choice for the presidency.

Although Finley was a poor orator, he was an energetic and able administrator and teacher. Like all the early Presidents, he devoted much of this time to teaching and gave instruction in Latin, Greek, and Hebrew. And like them too, he was overworked. He died in Philadelphia and was one of the few Presidents who was not buried in the Presidents' Row on Witherspoon Street.

(From a portrait attributed to Samuel F. B. Morse which was painted after the portrait by John Hesselius. It is reproduced by courtesy of Sidney E. Morse, Esq., the owner, and the Frick Art Reference Library.)

JOHN WITHERSPOON 1768-1794

JOHN WITHERSPOON became the sixth President, after refusing at first to leave his native Scotland. A descendant of John Knox and a brilliant scholar, he was graduated from the University of Edinburgh in 1742.

As administrator, Witherspoon set the College on a sound financial basis, raising funds by touring the colonies. The faculty was expanded by calling several professors to Princeton, and the curriculum was widely broadened and the lecture system introduced. Philosophy was enlarged so as to include political science, and the study of French was also inaugurated.

Witherspoon won wide fame in America by taking an active part in the Revolutionary movement. Princeton thus acquired a strong Whig reputation. A member of the Continental Congress, he was one of the three Princeton signers of the Declaration of Independence. During the Revolution he performed various war services, and successfully administered the College despite the depredations committed by the enemy.

Under Witherspoon, Princeton was literally "a school of statesmen," and five of his own students were later delegates at the Constitutional Convention.

In his last years Witherspoon did not live in the President's House, but settled at Tusculum.

(From the portrait by Charles Willson Peale by courtesy of Independence Hall.)

Landmarks and Memorabilia

THE LOG COLLEGE at Neshaminy, Pennsylvania, founded about 1726, was a forerunner of Princeton. It was established by the Rev. William Tennent, local pastor and prominent leader in the evangelical group known as New Lights.

Although the College of New Jersey was not a continuation of the Log College, supporters of the latter entered the board of trustees and otherwise became prominent.

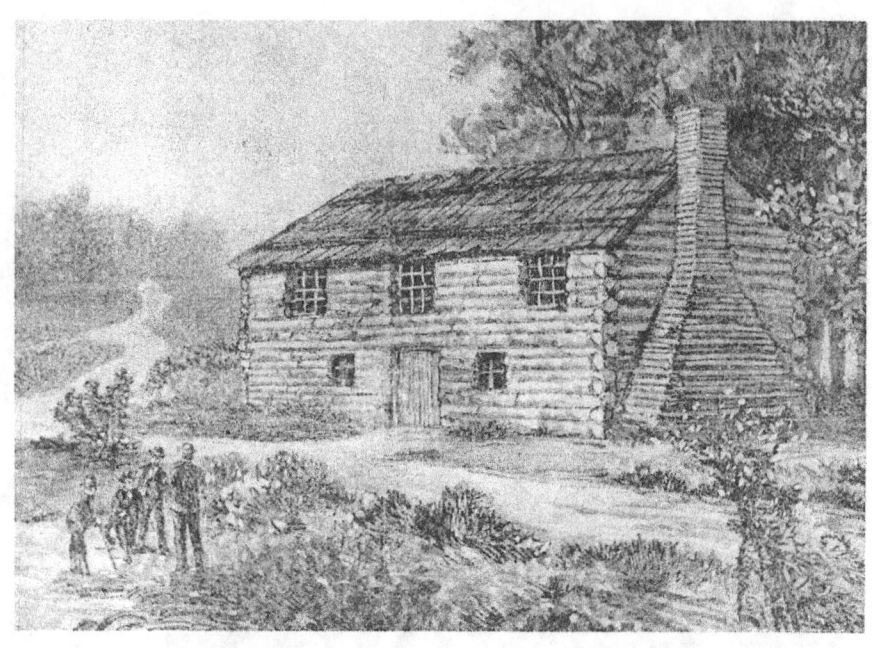

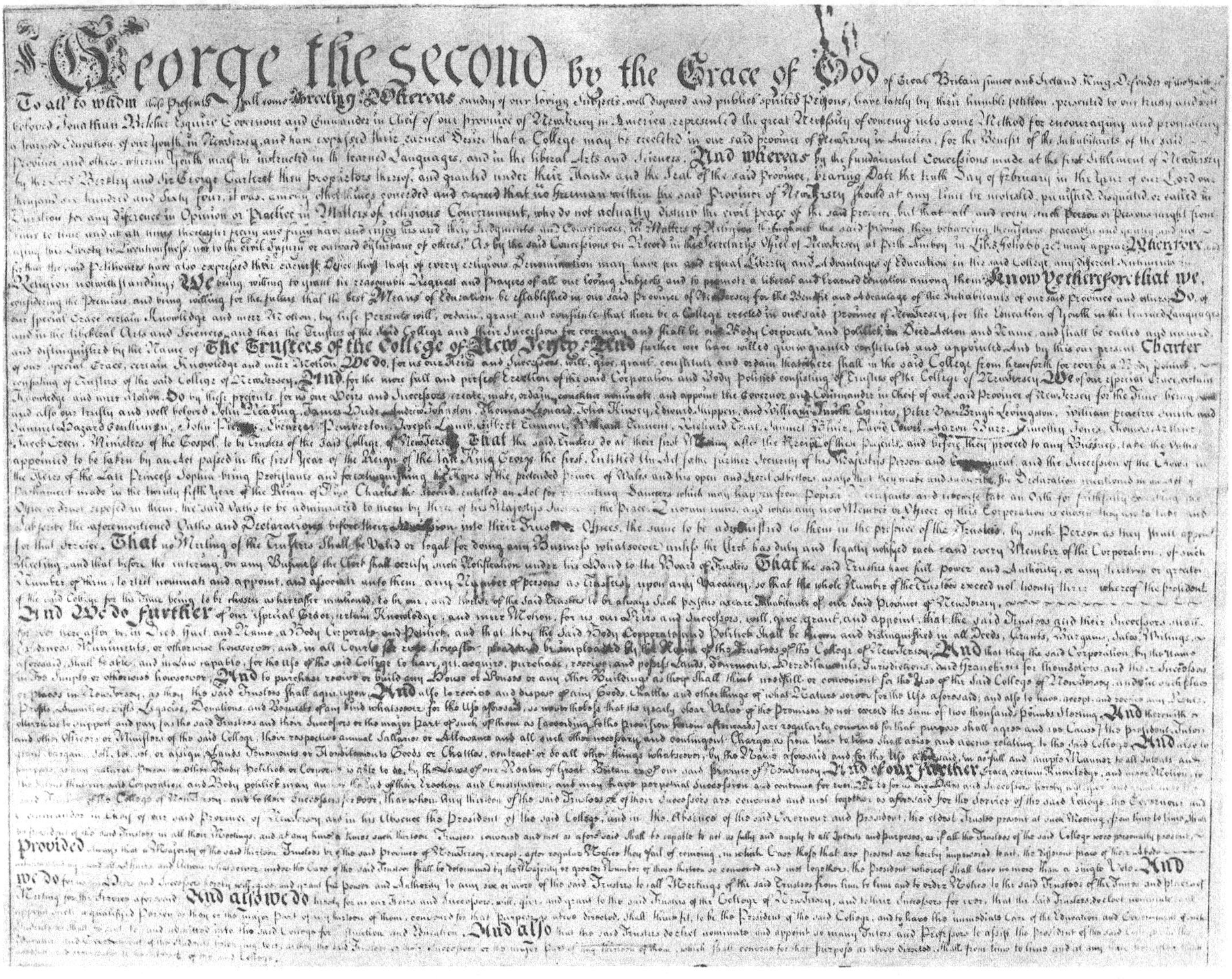
George the second by the Grace of God of Great Britain France and Ireland King Defender of the Faith &c.
To all to whom these Presents shall come Greeting: Whereas ...

The First Page of the Charter of 1748. The charter of 1746 was signed by John Hamilton when he was Acting Governor; and to avoid controversy the second charter was obtained under which Princeton operates today. The two charters were closely similar in wording, each specifying that the College was to be non-sectarian.

GEORGE II OF ENGLAND, in whose reign the College of New Jersey received its two charters. (This reproduction is from the portrait by Charles Jervas, court painter, that hangs in the Faculty Room. It replaces an earlier portrait of the King which was destroyed in the Battle of Princeton by a cannon-shot from Washington's army.)

GOVERNOR JONATHAN BELCHER, here depicted in the upper right hand corner, was the chief patron of the College of New Jersey. He signed the charter of 1748. Today he is principally remembered for his modest refusal to have Nassau Hall named after him. Princetonians are properly grateful to this Harvard graduate. (From the portrait by Franz Liopoldt owned by the Massachusetts Historical Society.)

GILBERT TENNENT, eldest son of the William Tennent who founded the Log College, became trustee of the College of New Jersey in 1747. His greatest service was his trip to England with Samuel Davies; the two were successful in raising funds for the construction of Nassau Hall.

November 21, 1748.   THE   NUMB. 305

NEW-YORK GAZETTE REVIVED IN THE WEEKLY POST-BOY.

With the freshest Advices   *Foreign and Domestick.*

Mr. Parker,

As the Acts of a publick Commencement are little known in these Parts, perhaps the following Relation from an Eye and Ear Witness, may be agreeable to many of your Readers.

ON Wednesday the ninth Instant, was held at *Newark,* the first Commencement of the College of *New Jersey*; at which was present his Excellency JONATHAN BELCHER. Esq; Governor and Commander in Chief of the said Province, and President of the Trustees, and sixteen Gentlemen, being other Trustees named in the Royal CHARTER: Who after they had all taken and subscribed the Oaths to the Government, and made and signed the Declaration which are appointed by divers Statutes of *Great Britain,* and had taken the particular Oath for the faithful Performance of their Trust, all which were required by the said Charter, they proceeded to the Election of a President of the said College ; whereupon the Reverend Mr. AARON BURR, was unanimously chosen.

Which being done, his Excellency was preceeded from his Lodgings at the President's House ; first by the Candidates walking in Couples uncovered ; next followed the Trustees two by two being covered, and last of all his Excellency the Governor, with the President at his Left Hand. At the Door of the Place appointed for the publick Acts, the Procession (amidst a great Number of Spectators there gathered) was inverted, the Candidates giving to the Right and Left Hand, and the Trustees in like Manner. His Excellency first entered with the President, the Trustees next following in the Order in which they were ranged in the Charter ; and last of all the Candidates. Upon the Bell ceasing, and the Assembly being composed, the President began the publick Acts by solemn Prayer to God in the *English* Tongue, for a Blessing upon the publick Transactions of the Day ; upon his Majesty King GEORGE the Second, and the Royal Family ; upon the *British* Nations and Dominions ; upon the Governor and Government of *New Jersey* ; upon all Seminaries of true Religion and good Literature ; and particularly upon the infant College of *New-Jersey.*

Which being concluded, the President attended in the Pulpit with the Reverend Mr. *Thomas Arthur,* who had been constituted Clerk of the Corporation, desired in the *English* Tongue, the Assembly to stand up and hearken to his Majesty's Royal CHARTER, granted to the Trustees of the College of *New Jersey.*

Upon which, the Assembly standing, the Charter was distinctly read by the Reverend Mr. *Arthur,* with the usual Indorsement by his Majesty's Attorney General, and the Certificate signed by the Secretary of the Province, of its having been approved in Council, with his Excellency's *Fiat* for the Province Seal, signed with his Excellency's own Hand.

After this, the Morning being spent, the President signified to the Assembly, that the succeeding Acts would be deferred till two o'Clock in the Afternoon.

Then the Procession, in Return to the President's House, was made in the Order before observed.

The like Procession being made in the Afternoon as in the Morning, and the Assembly being seated in their Places, and composed ; the President opened the publick Acts, first by an elegant Oration in the *Latin* Tongue, delivered *memoriter,* modestly declaring his Unworthiness of, and Unfitness for so weighty and important a Trust as had been reposed in him ; apologizing for the Defects that would unavoidably appear in his Part of the present Service ; displaying the manifold Advantages of the liberal Arts and Sciences, in exalting and dignifying the humane Nature, enlarging the Soul, improving its Faculties, civilizing Mankind, qualifying them for the important Offices of Life, and rendering Men useful Members of Church and State : That to Learning and the Arts, was chiefly owing the vast Preheminence of the polished Nations of *Europe,* to the almost brutish Savages of *America*; the Sight of which last was the constant Object of Horror and Commiseration. Then the President proceeded to mention the Honours paid by our Ancestors in *Great Britain,* to the Liberal Sciences ; by erecting and endowing those illustrious Seminaries of Learning, which for many Ages had been the Honour and Ornament of those happy Islands, and the Source of infinite Advantage to the People there : Observing, that the same noble Spirit had animated their Descendants, the first *English* Planters of *America*; who, as soon as they were formed into a civil State, in the very Infancy of Time, had wisely laid Religion and Learning at the Foundation of their Common wealth ; and had always regarded them as the firmest Pillars of their Church and State.——That hence very early arose *Harvard* College, in *New-Cambridge,* and afterwards *Yale* College, in *New-Haven,* which have now flourished with growing Reputation, for many Years, and have sent forth many hundreds of learned Men of various Stations and Characters in Life, that in different Periods have proved the Honour and Ornament of their Country ; and of which, the one or the other had been the ALMA MATER of most of the *Literati* then present. That Learning, like the Sun in its Western Progress, had now began to dawn upon the Province of *New Jersey,* through the happy Influence of its generous Patron their most excellent Governor ; who from his own Experience, and early Acquaintance with academic Studies, well knowing the Importance of a learned Education, and being justly sensible that in Nothing he could more subserve to the Honour and Interest of his Majesty's Government, and the real Good and Happiness of his Subjects in *New Jersey,* than by granting them the best Means to render themselves a *religious, wise,* and *knowing* People ; Had therefore, upon his happy Accession to his Government, made the Erection of a College in this Province, for the Instruction of Youth in the liberal Arts and Sciences, the immediate Object of his Attention and Care : The clearest Demonstration whereof they had by the Grant of his most gracious Majesty's Royal CHARTER in the Morning published in that Assembly, which had been conveyed to them through his Excellency's Hands ; which appears to have been founded in the noblest Munificence, granting the most ample Privileges consistent with the natural and religious Rights of Mankind, and calculated for the most extensive Good of all his Majesty's Subjects. That therein we see the Ax laid to the Root of that ANTICHRISTIAN BIGOTRY that had in every Age (wherever it had prevailed) been the Parent of Persecution, the Bane of Society, and the Plague of Mankind : That by the Tenour of his Majesty's Charter, it could assume no Place in the College of *New-Jersey*; but as a *foul Fiend,* was banish'd to its native Region, that *infernal* PIT from whence it sprung.

These, and many other Particulars having, *more Oratorio,* taken up about three Quarters of an Hour, and the printed *Theses* being dispersed among the Learned in the Assembly, the Candidates, by the Command of the President, entered upon the publick Disputations in *Latin* ; in which six Questions in Philosophy and Theology were debated. One of which was :

" *An Libertas agendi Secundum Dictamina Conscientiæ, in Rebus*
" *merè religiosis, ab ulla Potestate humana coerceri debeat ?*"

In *English,* Whether the Liberty of acting according to the Dictates of Conscience, in Matters merely religious, ought to be restrained by any humane Power ?

And it was justly held and concluded, That that Liberty ought not to be restrained. Then the President addressing himself to the Trustees in *Latin,* asked, Whether it was their Pleasure, that these young Men who had performed the publick Exercises in Disputation, should be admitted to the Degree of Batchelor of the Arts ?

Which being granted by his Excellency, in the Name of all the Trustees present, the President descended from the Pulpit ; being seated with his Head covered, received them two by two ; and according to the Authority to him committed by the Royal *Charter,* after the Manner of the Academies in *England,* admitted six young Scholars to the Degree of Batchelor of the Arts.

(Continued on page 16)

COURTESY OF THE NEW-YORK HISTORICAL SOCIETY

An Account of the First Commencement of the College of New Jersey, held at Newark in November 1748. The first graduating class comprised six members, of whom Richard Stockton became the most famous. (From *The New-York Gazette Revived in the Weekly Post-Boy*, Nov. 21, 1748.)

The Seal of the College was adopted in 1748, and was probably designed by William Peartree Smith. This trustee was a wealthy graduate of Yale, class of 1742, and the silversmith who did the engraving may have been Philip Goelet who did work for the Peartree family. This seal was used until 1896 when a new one was adopted.

Prospectus of the College, 1752. Several editions of this pamphlet were published to advertise the new institution and to appeal for funds. When Davies and Tennent were abroad on their trip to Britain, they had a new edition printed in London and two in Edinburgh in 1754.

PRÆSTANTISSIMO

Optima Eruditione, Dignitate ac Pietate sublimi, omnique fœlicissime gubernandi Ratione VIRO perillustri,

JONATHAN BELCHER, Armigero,

Provinciæ *Novæ-Cæsariæ* GUBERNATORI, Marisque contermini Vice-Admirallo,
Consummatissimo;---Nec non hujus Academiæ Patrono colendissimo;
Reverendo pariter ac honorando D. AARONI BURR, *Collegii Neo-Cæsariensis*, PRÆSIDI, Fidelissimis etiam
Ejusdem Curatoribus, Literatura ac Pietate conspicuis;

Vigilantissimis etiam, Ecclesiarum CHRISTI passim Pastoribus, Doctrina et Pietate adornatis;---Omnibus denique, Rei literariæ Cultoribus, de nostra Accademia bene merentibus, summa Gratitudine semper prosequendis; Hæc Philosophemata quæ (DEO Opt. Max. favente) sub Præsidis Moderamine sunt agitanda, Juvines Artibus initiati.

| Hugo Bay, | Alexander Clinton, | Jacobus Frielinghuysen, |
| Jacobus Beard, | Daniel Farrand, | Simeon Mitchel. |

Devotissima cum Observantia ac Humilitate,----D. D. D. C. Q.

THESES TECHNOLOGICÆ.
TECHNOLOGIA de omnium Artium ac Scientiarum generatim, regulis ac Terminis versatur.
1 Omnis Res Rhetoricæ est propria, quæ ornate dici, graviterque debeat.
2 Mentis Operationes & Termini quibus exprimuntur, adæquatum Logicæ Objectum, constituunt.
3 Algebra, Quantitatem Quæsitam, sive Numerum, sive Lineam, ut datum assumit.
4 Inter Trigonometriam planam & Sphæricam, quædam datur certa Relatio ac Harmonia.
5 Ergo accurata hujus Observatio, ad illam perdiscendam, multum conduceret.
6 Excellentia omnium Artium ac Scientiarum, a Tendentia ad Gloriam Dei & Hominum Fælicitatem promovendum, pendet.

THESES GRAMMATICÆ.
GRAMATICA, in quavis Lingua, Ideas Verbis apte & dilucide communicandi, Artem docet.
1 Sine Verbo expresso vel suppresso, Sententia esse nequit.
2 Grammatica per quam Lingua ignota docetur, Linguâ vernaculâ scribi debet.
3 Quo paucioribus Verbis quævis Lingua constat, eo facilius intelligi potest.
4 Cognitio Vocalium Mutationis, ad Linguam Hebraicam intelligendum, non est absolute necessaria.
5 Inter Hebræos Adverbium negandi sæpe intelligitur.
6 Hebræi, Gradum superlativum per Adverbium, exprimunt.
7 Omnium Linguarum Hebraica est antiquissima.

THESES RHETORICÆ.
RHETORICA est Ars Veritatem copiose et eleganter illustrandi.
1 Perlectio optimorum Authorum præsertim veterum Poetarum, ad Oratorem formandum, multum conducit.
2 Sine multum scribendo, Orator perfectus existere non potest.
3 Tamen Oratio sine Scriptis pronunciari debet.
4 Ordo, non minus Oratori quam Audientibus prodest.
5 Penitus Rei Cognitio, Memoriæ Lumen maxime adfert.
6 Vocis, Vultus, & Gestus, Moderatio cum Venustate, Orationem reddit jucundam.
7 Vox ultra Vires urgenda non est.

THESES LOGICÆ.
LOGICA est Ars, in Veritatem investigando ac aliis communicando, Ratione bene utendi.
1 Extensio & Comprehensio Idearum mutuo sese extendunt aut contrahunt.
2 Affirmatio Ideæ, Comprehensionem ejus, semper includit.
3 Differentia inter Species nominales, Differentiam inter reales, non arguit.
4 E Premissis particularibus, ad Conclusionem generalem, Consequentia non valet. Ergo,
5 In Premissis, unus Terminus universalis, majus quam in Conclusione semper esse debet.
6 Veræ Conclusiones a veris Principiis Oriuntur.
7 Ideæ simplices explicari non possunt.
8 Nomina, ad Ideas communicandas, non sunt absolute necessaria.
9 Ex diversis Ideis, eidem Nomini affixis, multarum Controversiarum oritur Causa.
10 Nomina particularia, cuivis Ideæ simplici annexa, Causam Erroris in Ideis communicandis sustulerent.
11 Sed hoc, quamvis Linguam, redderet nimis obscuram.

THESES MATHEMATICÆ.
MATHEMATICA, de, Quantitatis & ejus Relationum, Natura & Analogia tractat.
1 Circulus Triangulo est æqualis cujus Basis Peripheræ et Altitudo Radio sunt æquales.
2 In omni Parrallelogramate, duorum Diagonalium Quadrata, quatuor Laterum Quadrato sunt æqualia.
3 Privitivæ Quantitates, etsi realium sunt Defectus, tamen minores vel majores esse possunt.
4 Primitivæ positivis Quantitatibus, sunt heterogeneæ et vice versa. Ergo,
5 Inter positivas & primitivas Quantitates nulla datur Ratio.
6 In Hyperbola, Quadratum Axis conjugati, transversi Quadrato, ac Parameter Axi transverso, eandem habent Proportionem.
7 Sphæra Pyramidi est æqualis, cujus Basis Superficei, et Altitudo Sphæræ Radio ejus, sunt æqualia.
8 Pyramidum æqualium Basis & Altitudines, reciprocam habent Proportionem.
9 Sinus Arcuum similium, Radiis eorum, eandem habent Rationem.
10 Sphæræ Superficies, Circuli Areæ, ab ejus Radio descripti, est quadrupla.

THESES PHYSICÆ.
PHYSICA, Phænomenorum in Mundo Naturali secundum Leges Stabilitas Orientium, Solutionem indicat.
1 Altitudo Atmosphæræ, ob inæqualem Densitatem, accurate determinari nequit.
2 Inæqualis Atmosphæræ Densitas, partim ab ejus Elasticitate, oritur.
3 Vi Solis ac Lunæ attractiva, Fluxus ac Refluxus in Atmosphera, æque ac in Mari, efficitur.
4 Soni Velocitas Aeris Elasticitati est proportionalis. Ergo,
5 Cæteris paribus Æstate quam Hyeme est major.
6 Velocitas Lucis est 10210 major quam Terræ in ejus annua Orbita. Ergo,
7 Parrallaxis Syderum fixorum apparebit contrarie quam aliter esset.
8 Reflectio Radiorum Lucis, ab Atmosphera elastica, quamvis Particulam Lucis, circumambiente efficitur.
9 Corpusculum, in quavis Parte Sphæræ concavæ æque attractivæ, erit quietum.
10 In Divisione Sphæræ, solida Materia ut Cubi, Superficies autem ut Quadrata Diametrorum minuuntur. Ergo,
11 Corpora parva in Fluido, in Proportione solidæ Materiæ, magis quam majora resistuntur.
12 Retrocessio Poli Æquatoris circa Eclipticum, Solis ac Lunæ conjunctim Vi attractiva, efficitur.
13 Unde apparet Terram esse Figuræ Sphæroidalis.
14 Dies Solares, nec siderei Diebus nec sibi ipsis, sunt æquales.
15 Hujus Inæqualitatis, Revolutio Terræ circa Solem et eccliptica Orbitæ Figura sunt Causæ.
16 ☞ Omnia Phænomena, in Mundo naturali, immediatâ Dei Energiâ, efficiuntur.

THESES METAPHYSICÆ.
METAPHYSICA est, de Entibus in se abstracte consideratis, et eorum Causis, Generibus, ac Relationibus, Tractatus.
1 Subordinatio Causarum ad Infinitum procedere non potest.
2 Metaphysica Veritas & Perfectio Gradus not admittunt.
3 Perfectiones Dei morales, e Necessitate naturali, non exercentur.
4 Possibilitas naturalis absque Possibilitate morali existere potest.
5 Omnia, Necessitate Consequentiæ, sunt necessaria.
6 Sed hæc Necessitas, in Voluntatem Agentium moralium, nullam Influentiam habet.
7 ☞ Concia Successio cogitandi, ad personalem Identitatem constituendam, non est necessaria.

THESES ETHICÆ.
ETHICA, summam Fælicitatem per Praxin Virtutis, Rationem obtinendi docet.
1. Summum Bonum, in Fruitione Entis perfectissimi, constat.
2 Sine Respectu ad Deum, ut ultimum Finem, Actiones formaliter bonæ esse non possunt.
3 Judicium privatæ Discretionis, cuivis Agenti morali, est essentiale.
4 Sine Voluntatis Consensu Peccatum existere nequit. Ergo,
5 Libertatis Abusus Mali moralis fuit Origo.
6 Sine Virtute non potest esse alicujus Boni vera Fruitio.
7 Dictamina Rationis sunt iis Sensuum anteponenda.
8 In Statu Naturæ, (quibusdam Cognatis exceptis) quoad Imperium, Homines sunt æquales. Ergo,
9 Jus Regum, e Compacto Populi, originale Fundamen habuit. Ergo,
10 Competitor GEORGII Secundi (optimo Jure) nostri Regis, Imperium *Magnæ-Brittanniæ*, non minus injuste quam inaniter sibi vindicat.

His præcedit Oratio Salutatoria.

Habita in Comitiis academicis NOVARCÆ. in Nova-Cæsarea, Sexto Calendas Octobris, MDCCL.

Commencement Theses, 1750. Besides special orations, commencement exercises comprised "scholastic disputations" by the prospective bachelors, all carried on in Latin. Commencement was an ordeal for all hands.

John Shippen Dr
1752 May 2 To Cash for Shoes ... 0 8 0
To Plato Dialogue 8 6
To Cash 4 0
To Cash 2 6
To Cash 0 1 0
To Cash 1 6
To Cash 2 0
To French Schooling
To Cash for Horse

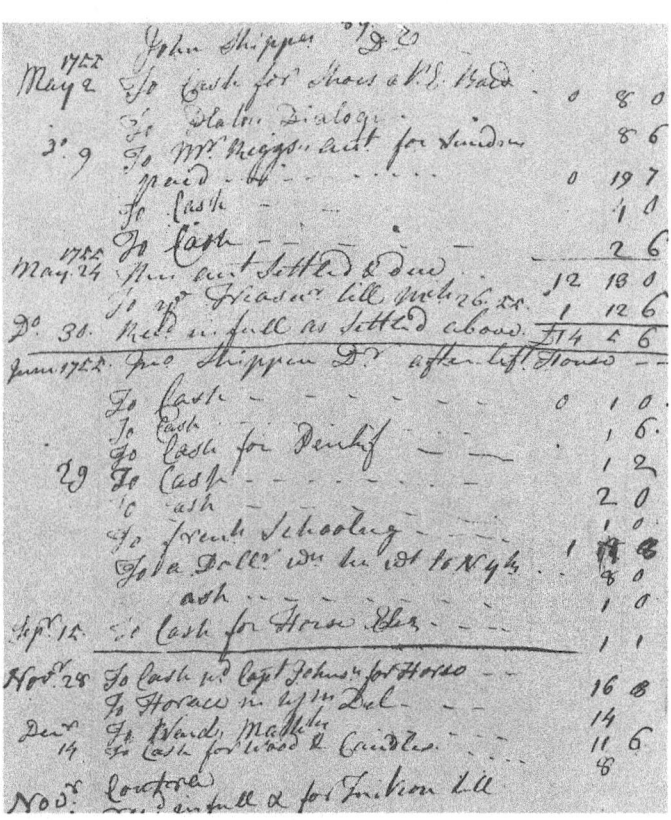

A Page from President Burr's Account Book. The expenditures of each student were carefully regulated.

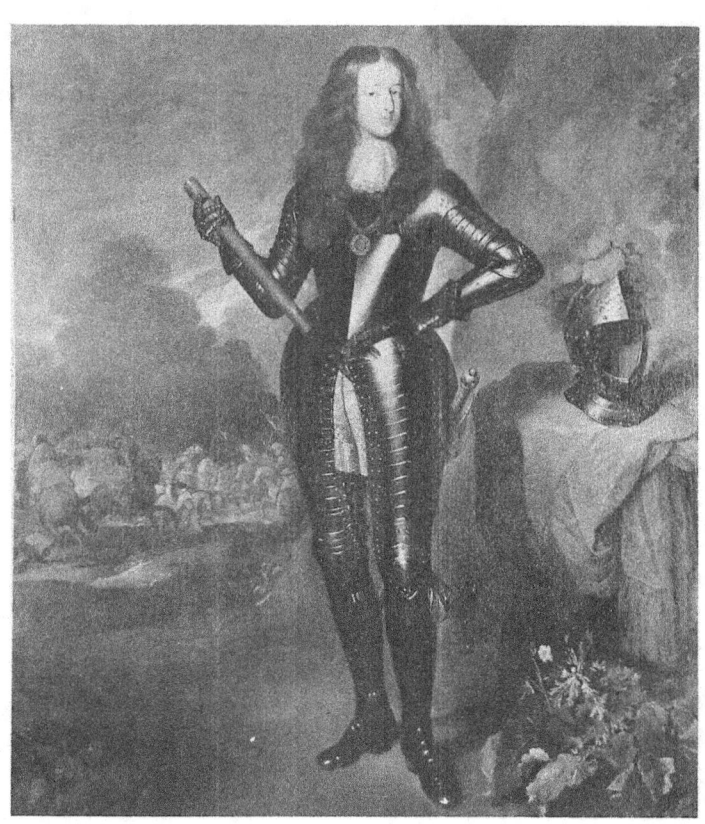

WILLIAM III, Prince of Orange-Nassau, for whom Nassau Hall was named. (From the portrait by Caspar Netscher.)

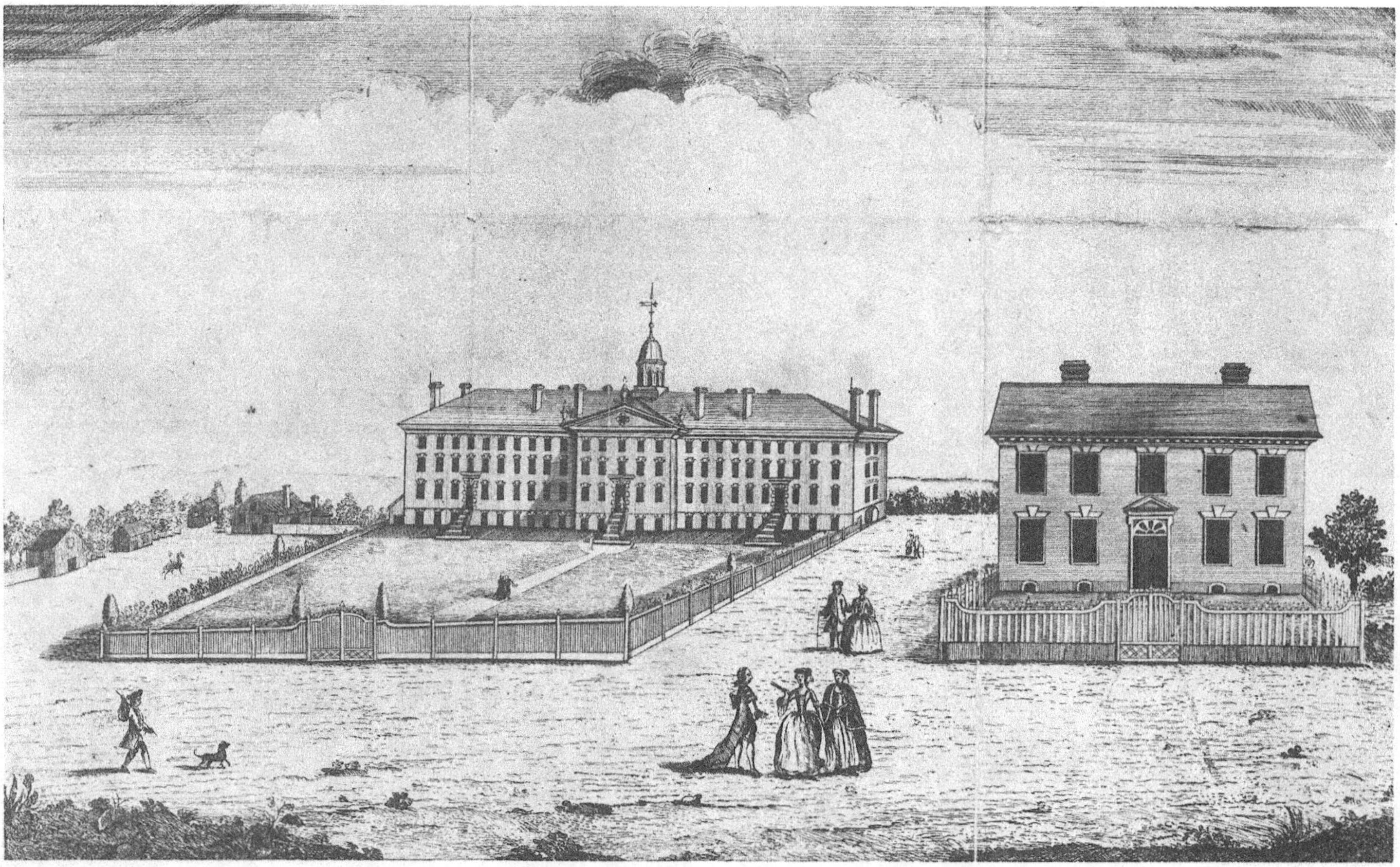

The Dawkins Engraving of 1764. This famous engraving was made from a sketch drawn by one of the Tennents. Incidentally the fence in front of Nassau Hall, shown here, never existed; and one wonders at the hills at the left.

The First Print of Nassau Hall, 1760. This engraving appeared in the *New American Magazine*, in March 1760. The editor, in the accompanying article, declared that only intense interest in the College warranted the cost.

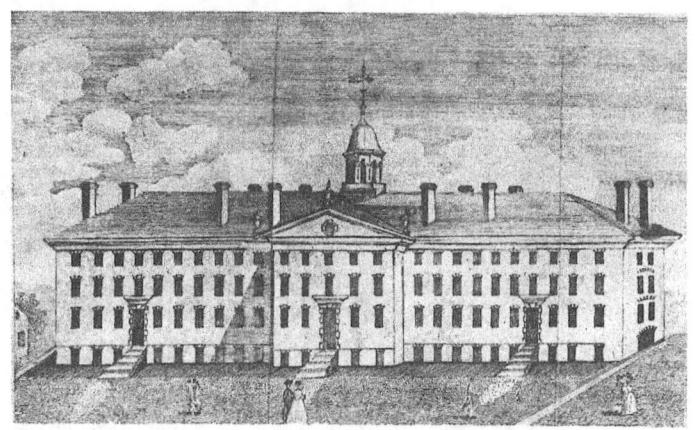

The Doolittle Engraving of Nassau Hall. It was made by Amos Doolittle, probably in 1776. He was a Connecticut Yankee who engraved portraits and historical scenes, of which the best known deal with the Revolution.

Although the College severely punished students who engaged in games of chance, officials saw no harm in holding a lottery for the benefit of the College. New Jersey frowned upon Princeton's lotteries, but other colonies were more open-minded. Hence this lottery in Delaware in 1772. The proceeds constituted fifteen per cent of the prize money. Several lotteries were held, the good Presbyterians apparently having few scruples when they got the proceeds.

Connecticut, despite its "blue laws," permitted a lottery for the benefit of the College of New Jersey in 1753. It resulted in a fair profit. The irregular cutting and design of the tickets, on the left side, was devised to make forgery difficult. The modern word, indenture, comes from this practice.

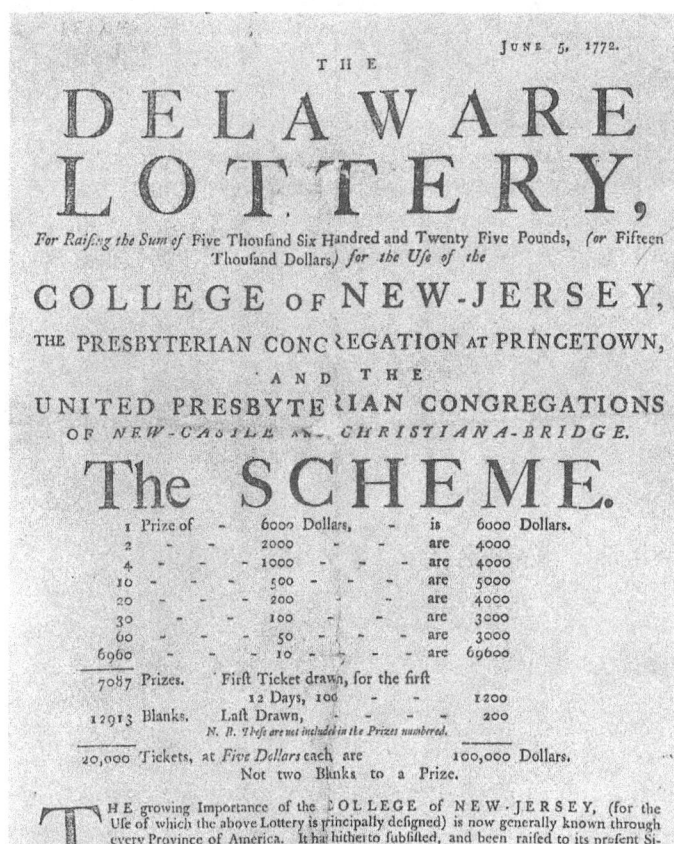

The First Catalogue of the Library. The first Library books were those of Presidents Dickinson and Burr. The real founder was Governor Belcher who gave his large collection.

Bachelor of Arts Diploma, 1764. The early diplomas were large and made of parchment. The diploma ribbon, to which the seal of the College was attached, was pink if the graduate was a member of Clio, blue if he belonged to Whig. William Woodhull became a leading Jersey clergyman with a flair for politics.

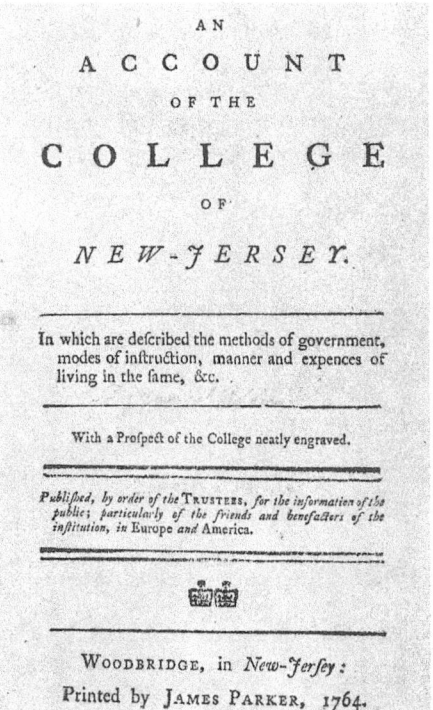

This pamphlet, the first history of Princeton, was written by Samuel Blair, a tutor, in 1764. He wrote that Nassau Hall produced graduates "of solid and rational piety."

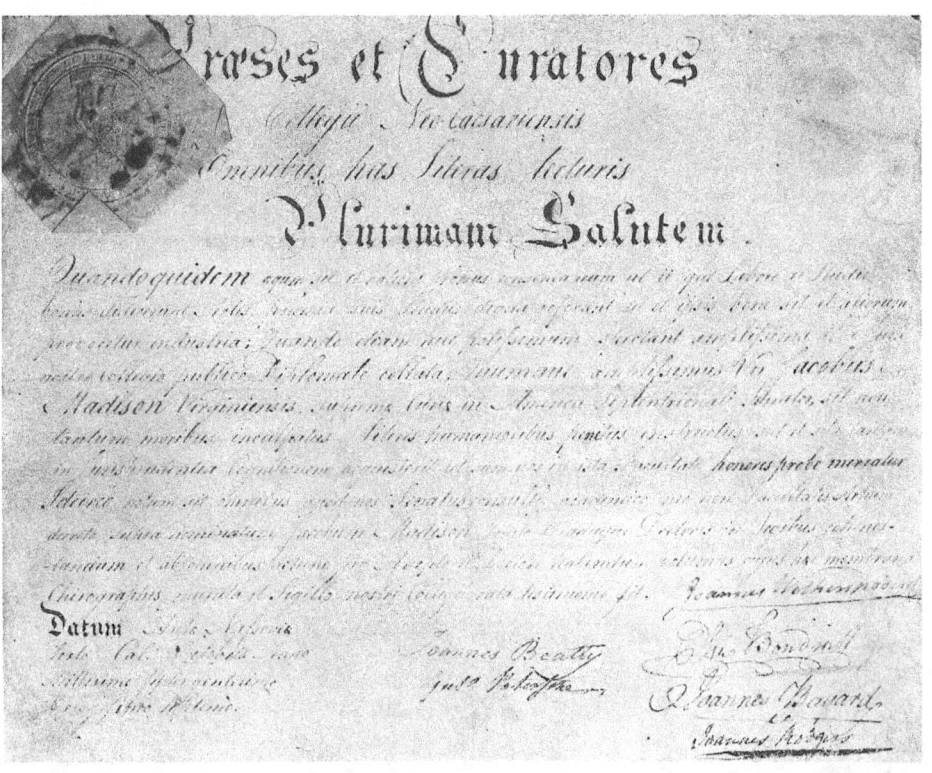

Doctor of Laws Diploma, 1787. The diplomas for honorary degrees were even larger than those for bachelors. The College of New Jersey gave an honorary degree in 1748 at its first commencement. James Madison 1771 received the degree of Doctor of Laws in 1787, after attending the Constitutional Convention.

Whereas it is represented to the Inhabitants of Princeton & its Neighbourhood that the Members of the Hon.ble Congress stand in Need of further Accommodations, & they being desirous to testify their respect for the Supreme Legislature of America & their wishes for their honouring New Jersey with their Residence, have agreed to furnish their best in their Power as follows, for One Year, or during the Winter, Viz.t Monday October 13.th 1783.

Names	Houses to let for One Year	Rooms with Fire Places	Rooms without Chimneys	Beds & Bedding	Breakfasts & Teas	Ditto & Dinners	Stables, Horses at Hay & Oats
The Rev.d D.r Witherspoon	1	Three		three	three		any number
The Rev. D.r Smith	2	Two		two	two		
Rob.t Stockton	3						
Tho.s Stockton	4	1		1	1		
M.r Moody	5						
M.rs Skelton	6						
C.t Moore	7	two		two	2		several
M.rs Rock	8	One		two	2		
M.r Sexton	9						
M.r Vanvorhees	10	three		three	3		
M.r Kelsey	11	two		two	2		
M.r M.c Comb	12	two		two	2		
M.r Harrison	13	three two	One	3	6	6	
M.r Stout	14	two		two	2		several
M.r Bushman	15	two		two	2		two

Princeton's housing shortage is nothing new. In 1783, when Congress was in session in Nassau Hall, a survey of rooms was made. The survey, preserved in the Library of Congress, was too disappointing, and Congress left.

Although not a Princeton graduate, few alumni had closer Princeton connections than ELIAS BOUDINOT who was for forty-nine years (1772-1821) a trustee. He early studied law with Richard Stockton and became an ardent devotee of the Revolutionary cause. In the war he acted as commissary-general of prisoners. He also served in the Continental Congress, and in 1782 was chosen the third "President of the United States in Congress Assembled." He held this office when Congress was in session at Nassau Hall. (From the Charles Willson Peale portrait in the Faculty Room.)

The Princeton Packet was the town's first newspaper, in 1786. It proudly bore a woodcut of Nassau Hall.

Alumni of the Early Period

EVERY educational institution takes credit for the success of its illustrious alumni; it ignores the failures and dismisses the dour comment of Adam Smith that it is difficult for a promising undergraduate not to improve a great deal in four years no matter where he may be.

The record compiled by the first forty classes of the College of New Jersey was an amazing one. Admittedly undergraduates in the eighteenth century, before the days of mass education, were a sharply selected group. Moreover the College was truly national in the composition of its student body, for they came from New England and the South as well as the middle colonies and states. Although most of the early alumni entered the ministry, it was politics and public affairs in which they won their greatest fame. The signature of Witherspoon on the Declaration of Independence was accompanied by those of two Princeton graduates; and in the Constitutional Convention there were nine Princeton alumni, all taking a prominent part in the debates.

The seventeen alumni whose portraits are reproduced in the following pages were the leaders in their respective professions, but the list could have been much more inclusive. Here, representative of the alumni of the early period, are eight statesmen and lawyers, two soldiers, three educators who were also ministers, two doctors, one man of letters, and one businessman.

COURTESY OF THE BOWDOIN COLLEGE MUSEUM OF FINE ARTS

JAMES MADISON 1771; from the famous portrait by Gilbert Stuart. The fourth President of the United States was the outstanding example of the scholar and statesman graduated at Princeton under Witherspoon. Author of the Virginia Plan, he was justly called "the father of the Constitution." In his career as Secretary of State and war President, he encountered an international situation which was a historical parallel to that faced by President Wilson a century later.

RICHARD STOCKTON 1748; from the Princeton portrait attributed to John Wollaston. Prominent Revolutionary leader in New Jersey, he signed the Declaration of Independence.

WILLIAM PATERSON 1763; from the Princeton portrait by Edward L. Mooney. This famous lawyer presented the New Jersey Plan before the Constitutional Convention.

COURTESY OF YALE UNIVERSITY ART GALLERY

OLIVER ELLSWORTH 1766; from a miniature by John Trumbull. A proposer of the famous Connecticut Compromise, he was later Chief Justice of the United States.

LUTHER MARTIN 1766. Maryland's leading lawyer, he opposed the Constitution in the Convention. Later, he successfully defended Aaron Burr in his trial for treason.

OWNED BY THE NEW-YORK HISTORICAL SOCIETY

AARON BURR 1772; from the portrait by John Vanderlyn. The first graduate to become Vice President, this fascinating politician was a rival to Hamilton and Jefferson.

OWNED BY THE NEW-YORK HISTORICAL SOCIETY

AARON OGDEN 1773; from the portrait by Asher B. Durand. Soldier and politician, he unwittingly secured freedom of interstate commerce in the case of *Gibbons v. Ogden*.

EDWARD LIVINGSTON 1781. A master of jurisprudence, he became both Mayor of New York and Secretary of State. He wrote many of Jackson's important state papers.

THE HISTORICAL SOCIETY OF PENNSYLVANIA

JOSEPH REED 1757. He served in the Revolution as Washington's military secretary, and helped plan the attack on Princeton. Later he was executive of Pennsylvania.

HENRY LEE 1773. Light-Horse Harry Lee was the great cavalry leader whose campaigns in the South proved him a master strategist. Later he became Governor of Virginia.

UNIVERSITY OF PENNSYLVANIA

JOHN EWING 1754; from the portrait by E. D. Marchant. A tutor in Nassau Hall, he later became provost of the University of Pennsylvania and a leading theologian.

BROWN UNIVERSITY

JAMES MANNING 1762; from the portrait by Cosmo Alexander. The founder and first President of Brown University, he was an outstanding educator and minister.

SAMUEL KIRKLAND 1765. A missionary to the Six Nations in New York, he served as a chaplain in the Revolution. In 1793 he became the founder of Hamilton College.

WILLIAM SHIPPEN 1754. The son of the co-architect of Nassau Hall, this distinguished doctor founded the medical school of the University of Pennsylvania.

BENJAMIN RUSH 1760; from the portrait attributed to John Neagle. A signer of the Declaration of Independence, he became the nation's greatest medical teacher and doctor.

PHILIP FRENEAU 1771. The roommate of James Madison, the "Poet of the Revolution" entered politics as a pamphleteer to defend Jefferson and Madison against Hamilton.

JACOBUS (JAMES) ROOSEVELT 1780. A leading New York businessman and lawyer, Roosevelt engaged in sugar refining and West Indian trade, and banking and real estate.

The Middle Period 1795-1888

THE MIDDLE PERIOD of Princeton's history comprises the century between the death of Witherspoon and Patton's administration when the College officially became Princeton University. It was an era in which the institution, facing bright prospects at first, slipped badly and then began a slow climb that was climaxed by the brilliant administration of James McCosh.

Although the death of Witherspoon marked the end of an era, there was no serious interruption in Princeton's everyday life. His son-in-law, Samuel Stanhope Smith, then serving as Vice President, was the unanimous choice of the trustees.

Smith's administration was one of mixed success and failure. In 1802 the College suffered a severe blow in the burning of Nassau Hall. Fortunately efforts to obtain funds for its rebuilding met with ready response; the restoration fund was so large as to permit the construction of two additional buildings. These were the Philosophical Building and Stanhope Hall (originally called the Library); harmonizing with Nassau Hall, they balanced the front campus.

Of advanced views in education, Smith was unfortunate in that he was rigorously controlled by a board of trustees whose views were far from liberal. Most of them were ministers who insisted that the College turn out pious young men, and who had little concept of Princeton as a national institution. The faculty was closely watched for any signs of unorthodox opinion. Teaching efficiency fell as the members became overworked—the number of undergraduates was now about one hundred and fifty. Student morale suffered while the tutors vainly attempted to enforce discipline. In 1807 came the great rebellion when the student body locked itself in Nassau Hall in protest against the suspension of three of their number. The trustees, blaming irreligion and dissipation as the cause of the trouble, did not realize that disorders, then current at other colleges besides Princeton, were a phenomenon that accompanied the trend toward the secularization of education. It was shortly after this time that the general assembly of the Presbyterian Church, disappointed with the College of New Jersey, founded the Princeton Theological Seminary.

In 1812 President Smith resigned and was followed by Ashbel Green, a minister and former faculty member who had been a critic of Smith's "laxness." Green's administration was one of almost continuous turmoil. In 1814 came the explosion of the "great cracker," a log charged with gunpowder, which cracked the front walls of Nassau Hall. And in 1817 the students in Nassau Hall barricaded themselves, nailed up the doors of the tutors and woke a peaceful Sunday morning with cries of "Rebellion."

In 1823 Green was succeeded by James Carnahan, whose administration was to be the longest in Princeton's history. Disorders continued in the early part of his regime, and the number of students dropped so sharply that the faculty was forced to a more lenient policy. At the low point the College had only seventy-one undergraduates. Slowly, however, Princeton made its way up from this ebb tide in its fortunes. Of great importance was the formation of the Alumni Association of Nassau Hall in 1826 "to promote the interests of the College and the friendly intercourse of its graduates." The venerable James Madison was its first president. Not only did the alumni give funds with which to employ more inspiring teachers, but gradually they were able to secure a voice in the College's educational policies. It was they who "brought about the secularizing of Princeton, the gradual weakening of denominational control." With the appointment of new faculty members such as Joseph Henry and John Torrey, Princeton gathered strength in the 1830's and at its centennial could view the future with confidence.

The Vice President during most of Carnahan's regime was John Maclean, conscientious if somewhat undignified administrator who was largely responsible for the building up of the faculty. Upon Carnahan's retirement in 1854 he served for fourteen years. By the time of the Civil War the number of students had reached three hundred; and although the departure of the southern undergraduates was a severe blow, the College later resumed its natural growth. He retired to write "The History of the College of New Jersey."

In 1868 the trustees, mindful of the action taken a century before, secured another Scot to take charge of the College. James McCosh, like Witherspoon, proved an administrator ranking at the top of Princeton's long list. Favored with large bequests from the Green family and other generous benefactors, McCosh directed a vast expansion in which Princeton's intellectual life was broadened and its physical plant practically doubled.

Of greatest importance was the strengthening of the faculty by the selection of young men of promise who later developed into outstanding scholars. As earlier, the most famous names were in the sciences and were to win for Princeton an international reputation. By the end of McCosh's administration, the growing emphasis upon research and scholarship, the increase in graduate work, and the establishment of the Schools of Science and of Art had made Princeton a university in all but name. President McCosh was never able to secure that nominal distinction for his College, but the credit for the change was largely his. In 1888 he retired in his seventy-eighth year, beloved by all Princeton men.

The Presidents

SAMUEL STANHOPE SMITH was the first graduate of the College of New Jersey to become President. The salutatorian of the class of 1769, he had been a tutor in Nassau Hall and then, moving to Virginia, had been a founder and the first rector of Hampden-Sydney. He returned to Princeton in 1779 to become professor of moral philosophy. He married Ann Witherspoon and was the unanimous choice of the trustees to succeed his father-in-law. For some years the good doctor, quite blind, had been living at Tusculum, and the affairs of the College had been administered by Smith who served as Vice President. With the election of Smith, incidentally, the salary of the President was for the first time designated in coinage of the United States, being fixed at fifteen hundred dollars a year.

Although a theologian, Smith had a natural interest in science. He himself wrote a distinguished paper, his *Essay on the Causes of the Variety of Complexion and Figure in the Human Species,* one of the early efforts to apply evolutionary ideas to mankind. He encouraged the study of chemistry and admitted special students to scientific courses.

Unfortunately Smith's advanced ideas did not receive the support of the trustees; he resigned in 1812.

(From the portrait by Charles B. Lawrence in the Faculty Room.)

SAMUEL STANHOPE SMITH 1795-1812

ASHBEL GREEN was the valedictorian of the class of 1783 and had numerous Princeton antecedents. His father, the Reverend Jacob Green, was one of the trustees under the second charter; his grandfather, the Reverend John Pierson, had been one of the seven founders; and his great-grandfather, Abraham Pierson, had been a founder of Yale and its first President. Green himself had served both as trustee and faculty member at Princeton.

Unfortunately these contacts with the past symbolized Green's own attitude. A stern Calvinist who regarded Harvard's growing Unitarianism with horror, he was out of touch with the liberal trends in education. He hoped for a religious revival among the undergraduates, but his administration was to be one of almost continuous turmoil caused by student riots.

The college year of 1816-1817 was the most turbulent, being marked by the "great rebellion" in which the students barricaded themselves in Nassau Hall in a general protest against the length of reading assignments. When fourteen students were dismissed without any specific evidence against them, rioting continued with the result that seven more offenders were arrested and held for trial in the courts.

In 1822 Green resigned and returned to the ministry in Philadelphia, where he was more successful. A conscientious conservative, he was out of harmony with the times.

(From the portrait by Wooley in the Faculty Room.)

ASHBEL GREEN 1812-1822

JAMES CARNAHAN became President when the College of New Jersey was in a precarious situation. The number of students had dropped to about eighty, income was small, and there was almost no endowment; moreover, the trustees were divided. The presidency had been offered to the able Vice President, Philip Lindsley, but he, despairing of Princeton's future and uncertain of his backing, had rejected it to head the University of Nashville.

Carnahan had been salutatorian in the class of 1800, had entered the ministry, and had founded and administered successfully an academy at Georgetown, D. C.

Although known as the "Boss," Carnahan was a good deal of a figurehead. Yet he did not block progressive policies which were promoted by others; and he was fortunate in having John Maclean, elected Vice President in 1829, carry out much of the administrative detail.

The problem of discipline remained of paramount importance in the early days, but slowly the fortunes of the College turned for the better. The funds raised by the new Alumni Association of Nassau Hall were used to employ outstanding faculty members, and to build East and West Colleges and the Halls for the Cliosophic and American Whig Societies. When President Carnahan resigned in 1854, the tribulations of thirty years before had been forgotten.

(From the portrait by Edward L. Mooney in the Faculty Room.)

JAMES CARNAHAN 1823-1854

JOHN MACLEAN was a thorough Princetonian by birth and environment. The son of the College's first professor of chemistry, he was born in Princeton and was graduated in the class of 1816 as its youngest member. In 1818 he became a tutor, and during the next forty years he taught such varied subjects as mathematics, natural philosophy, Latin, Greek, and the evidences of Christianity. He was elected Vice President in 1829, and succeeded President Carnahan in 1854.

Maclean was neither a brilliant scholar nor a great teacher, but no President gave more time to his duties. He almost literally ran Princeton single-handed, for at that time the office included the functions of registrar, secretary, proctor, and chaplain. He knew every student by name, gave personal advice or warning, and visited and prayed when needed. His main fault was a lack of dignity which became evident when he tried to quiet a horn spree or attempted personally to apprehend some offender.

During his administration, some $450,000 was received by the College, a sum greater than the total of all previous gifts. He successfully administered the institution despite such setbacks as the fire of 1855 and the Civil War; a third of the students came from the South and the campus was depleted during the war. He retired in 1868, and wrote the first detailed history of his beloved College.

(From the portrait by Edward L. Mooney in the Faculty Room.)

JOHN MACLEAN 1854-1868

JAMES McCOSH 1868-1888

JAMES McCOSH became the eleventh President of Princeton in 1868, a century after another Scotsman, John Witherspoon, had been called to Princeton. And just as the latter had been the greatest President of the eighteenth century, so McCosh was in the nineteenth.

During his regime gifts totalling about three millions of dollars were received, and physically the College underwent a vast expansion. Fourteen buildings were added to the nine standing on his arrival. Most notable among the new additions were the School of Science, Chancellor Green Library, Dickinson Hall, several dormitories, the Museum of Historic Art, the Bonner Gymnasium, and Marquand Chapel. It was unfortunate, of course, that this great building program coincided with a period of poor architectural taste.

As the endowment increased, the size of the faculty was trebled. In his inaugural address, McCosh had chosen as his subject, "On Academic Teaching in Europe"; and the ideas of scholarship and teaching expressed therein were well exemplified in the distinguished scholars whom McCosh called to Princeton. The general intellectual atmosphere was so stimulated as to lead to a large growth in graduate study. The Graduate Department was formally organized in 1877, and such degrees as Doctor of Philosophy, Doctor of Science, and Doctor of Literature were now granted.

Under McCosh the number of undergraduates rose from about 250 to 600. A modified elective system was introduced, but President McCosh wisely refused to introduce such an extreme policy in this respect as was advocated by President Eliot of Harvard. President McCosh encouraged the students to engage in athletics, and the construction of a gymnasium was one of his first objectives. Intercollegiate sports became well established at this time, the first football game with Rutgers taking place in 1869. A compulsory gymnasium course for freshmen and sophomores was inaugurated in 1883, Princeton being preceded only by Amherst in demanding physical training for all.

When President McCosh retired in 1888, the old College of New Jersey had been transformed both in spirit and physical appearance. The trustees realized this and at the time of his death, six years later, they recorded in the minutes, "The results of his Presidency have made a new epoch in our history. The College has virtually become a University."

(From the portrait by John W. Alexander in the Faculty Room.)

PHILIP LINDSLEY 1804, was an outstanding educator of the early nineteenth century. For a decade he was the leading faculty member at Princeton, possessing both brilliance as a scholar and popularity with the students. It was a misfortune that he never became President.

His academic career was unusual. He was Greek and Latin tutor between 1807 and 1809, when he left to enter the ministry. In 1812 he returned as librarian, and the following year was made professor of languages and clerk of the board of trustees. In 1817 he became Vice President; and in 1822, after President Green's resignation, he was Acting President for a year.

During the turbulent days of Green's administration, Lindsley's advanced ideas on education and athletics for undergraduates could not prevail. The presidency was finally offered him in 1823; but knowing that he did not have the united support of the trustees, he rejected the offer to become head of the University of Nashville where he played a notable role in the educational life of the South.

Faculty Leaders

JOSEPH HENRY, who is usually accredited with the rank of Princeton's greatest scientist, became professor of natural philosophy in 1832. At Albany Academy he had already conducted research in the relation of electric currents to magnetism, and had devised a magnet with insulated wire.

In Princeton he continued his experiments, the most notable being in the field of telegraphy and in induced currents. He early set up a telegraph wire between his laboratory in Philosophical Hall and his house, on the site of Reunion. Over it he sent messages, including one that indicated when he wanted his lunch. His experiments with telegraphy antedated those of Morse. Independent of Faraday he discovered and experimented with induced currents. The students were especially impressed with the huge magnet which he constructed; it was so powerful that it could lift "twenty-five sneezing and coughing" undergraduates.

In 1846 Henry left Princeton to become director of the Smithsonian Institution, but he frequently came back to give lectures. At Washington he played an all-important role as the first executive of organized science.

Much of Henry's apparatus is preserved in the museum in Palmer Physical Laboratory. Depicted on this page are Henry's static machine and his telegraph receiving set; the curved piece at the top of the latter is a striker which hit a bell when the circuit was closed. (The portrait is by Henry Ulke, in Palmer Physical Laboratory.)

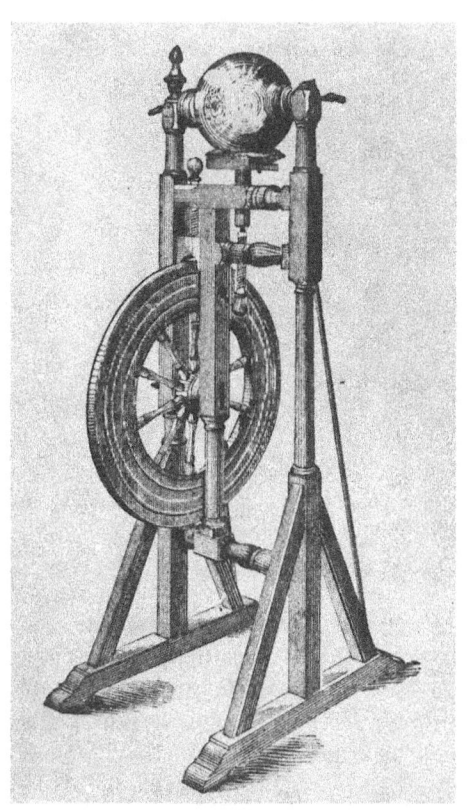
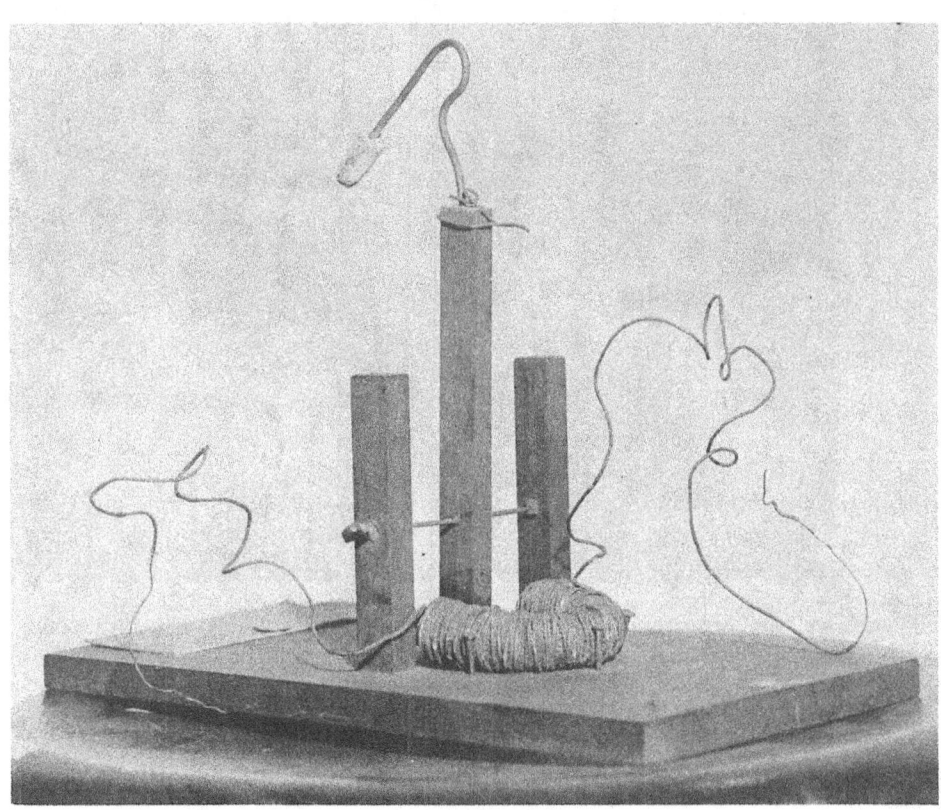

A "wireless" demonstration on the campus. Joseph Henry had experimented with induced currents at Albany Academy and he continued his research after coming to Princeton in 1832. In successive experiments on the campus, he was able to induce a current over two hundred feet away, even through the thick walls of Nassau Hall.

In this scene, part of a mural painted by Gifford R. Beal 1900 in the Engineering Building, Henry stands on the left. An assistant turns the handle of the static machine, behind which John Maclean, then Vice President, is standing. Between Henry and Maclean is Professor Albert B. Dod, famous mathematician.

JOHN MACLEAN, father of President Maclean, was the College's first professor of chemistry in 1795. His experiments, probably the first made in any American college, were "the wonder of Nassau Hall."

STEPHEN ALEXANDER, cousin of Joseph Henry, accompanied the latter to Princeton and became the first professor of astronomy. An outstanding teacher and scholar, he led several expeditions to observe eclipses.

ARNOLD HENRY GUYOT, Princeton's great geologist, became professor of geology and physical geography in 1854. He established the College's geological museum; and, with Joseph Henry, set up a system of meteorological stations.

JOHN TORREY had the distinction of holding professorships at Princeton and the College of Physicians and Surgeons simultaneously. One of the country's greatest botanists, he traveled widely to obtain specimens.

JAMES McCOSH arrived in Princeton in 1868 to take up his duties. At the President's House (now the Dean's House) he was met by an enthusiastic group of undergraduates.

McCosh was the last President to live there. He moved to Prospect in 1878.

First Faculty Group Picture, 1867-1868. John Maclean and professors standing in front of Professor Guyot's house. From left to right: John S. Schanck, Arnold H. Guyot, Charles W. Shields, Stephen Alexander, Henry C. Cameron, President Maclean, Lyman H. Atwater, John T. Duffield, and Charles A. Aiken.

PRESIDENT McCOSH AND PROFESSORS, 1870-1871. On the porch of the President's House, left to right: John T. Duffield, Lyman H. Atwater, President McCosh, Stephen Alexander, and Arnold H. Guyot.

Standing in front, left to right: Henry C. Cameron, James C. Welling, John S. Schanck, Charles W. Shields, William A. Packard, and Joseph Kargé.

PRESIDENT MCCOSH AND FACULTY, about 1873. This picture was made by imposing individual portraits upon the library background. From left to right: John T. Duffield, John S. Schanck, Arnold H. Guyot, Henry N. Van Dyke, President McCosh, Frederic Vinton, Henry C. Cameron, William A. Packard, John M. Cross, Stephen Alexander, George Goldie, Henry T. Eddy, Stephen G. Peabody, Cyrus F. Brackett, William McD. Halsey, Joseph Kargé, Lyman H. Atwater, Theodore W. Hunt, Henry B. Cornwall, James C. Moffat, Charles W. Shields, and John S. Hart.

Commencement Day, 1878. Until the building of Alexander Hall, commencement exercises were held in the Presbyterian Church. In this scene from *Leslie's Weekly* of July 6, 1878, President McCosh is handing out a diploma.

JAMES O. MURRAY, D.D. 1867, was the first of Princeton's deans, the office being created in 1883 to administer discipline. Despite his scholarly appearance, Dean Murray was a man of action, capable of ending any riot.

CYRUS FOGG BRACKETT was called to Princeton by President McCosh to hold the new chair in physics named for Joseph Henry. In 1889 he established the first Department of Electrical Engineering in the country.

CHARLES A. (Twinkle) YOUNG was Princeton's leading astronomer, succeeding Stephen Alexander in 1877. His nickname came from his twinkling eyes, not from the stars. His *The Sun* went through several editions.

JOHN B. MCMASTER was one of the greatest of American historians. Curiously enough, he was an instructor in civil engineering when in 1883 he produced volume one of "*A History of the People of the United States.*"

ALLAN MARQUAND 1874. Appointed professor of art in 1882, he organized the Department of Art and Archaeology. A great art scholar, he started the Princeton monographs with his "Della Robbias in America."

Buildings and Views

STANHOPE HALL. Built in 1803, it did not receive its modern name (in honor of Samuel Stanhope Smith) until 1915. It was earlier known as the Library, Geological Hall, and the College Offices. On the east side of Nassau Hall, Philosophical Hall was erected as a counterpart to Stanhope. This view was taken in the 1860's.

EAST COLLEGE was the first building to be used exclusively as a dormitory. Constructed in 1833 on the site of the Pyne Library, it was torn down to make way for the latter. Many alumni regarded the act of demolition as the "Crime of '97," for it destroyed the balance of the back campus. This view was taken in 1883.

WEST COLLEGE was built in 1836 as a counterpart to East College, each facing the other across the back campus. Its cost was only $13,000. It was remodeled in 1926 and for years the ground floor has been occupied by the University Store. This picture was made in 1894 and reveals in the foreground Jimmy Johnson, famous vendor of candy.

THE JOSEPH HENRY HOUSE was built in 1838 for the famous physicist. This view was taken in 1863, seven years before it was moved to make way for Reunion. In 1925 it was moved again to make way for the Chapel, and in 1946 it was moved from the north-east corner of the campus to its present resting place on the front campus.

WHIG HALL. The original Halls of the American Whig and Cliosophic Societies were built in 1837-1838, much to the relief of the members who had earlier used cramped quarters in Nassau Hall and then Stanhope. The halls were copied from a temple on the Island of Teos, while their columns were from the temple on the Ilissus.

The Princeton Campus, about 1840. This lithograph by J. H. Bufford best reveals the second Nassau Hall as reconstructed by Benjamin H. Latrobe after the fire of 1802. The Halls of the Whig and Cliosophic Societies were then located at the ends of the sidewalks, and the front and the back campus were in quite even balance.

THE OLD CHAPEL. The old prayer hall in Nassau Hall was the first chapel for undergraduates. In 1847 a Chapel was erected on the east side of Nassau Hall, although some trustees, finding the building was cruciform, deeply resented this intrusion of "popery" on the campus. For many years the drab little building was "regarded with aversion." This view was taken in 1862. The Old Chapel was demolished in 1897 to make way for the Pyne Library.

INTERIOR OF OLD CHAPEL. The furore over the cruciform shape was carried over to the organ, a few conservatives protesting against an instrument so "worldly." This view shows the Chapel in unusually good repair, for students soon notched the seats with initials and slogans.

THE REFECTORY. Students first ate in the basement of Nassau Hall, and then in Philosophical Building. In mid-century, this ancient house on William Street was used as a refectory. This picture, taken in 1862, shows a few hungry students waiting for lunch.

THE LAW SCHOOL, 1847-1855. The opening of the Princeton Law School coincided with the Centennial celebration. The building was constructed by Richard S. Field 1821 who became one of the three professors on the faculty. Through lack of students, the School was discontinued in 1855. The building was later used as a railroad office, an upperclass clubhouse, and as the residence of the organist of Trinity Church. Known today as Ivy Hall, its name was taken by the Ivy Club which once rented it.

A. W. RICHARDS

VIEW OF NASSAU HALL,

THE FRONT CAMPUS, about 1860. Nassau Hall burned a second time, in 1855, and was restored by John Notman, Philadelphia architect. He had earlier erected Prospect and other Florentine buildings, and the Italian influence is best seen in the two central arches and the towers at the ends. The towers were removed in 1905, largely through the influence of Moses Taylor Pyne 1877; Princetonians would today agree that it was not the least of his many services to the University.

(From the lithograph by Robertson, Seibert and Shearman.)

FIRST GYMNASIUM, 1859-1865. Princeton's first gymnasium was a barn-like structure, built near the site of Witherspoon. Students paid half of its cost. In 1865 it was set afire after a tramp with yellow fever slept there overnight.

BONNER GYMNASIUM. This chateau-like structure was built in 1869 and was the gift of Robert Bonner and Henry G. Marquand, New York philanthropists. Unlike some college presidents, James McCosh encouraged athletics, and the Bonner Gymnasium was the first large gymnasium to be built by any American college. It was located just west of the site of Alexander Hall, a special lot being acquired for it. The view below shows the interior, with a group of undergraduates proudly displaying the limited apparatus of that day. Gymnastics became one of the most popular sports.

THE LIBRARY IN NASSAU HALL, 1856-1873. After the fire of 1855 the library was moved over from Stanhope.

THE E. M. MUSEUM OF GEOLOGY AND ARCHAEOLOGY, in Nassau Hall, after the building of Chancellor Green Library.

FIRST VIEW OF THE P. J. & B., in 1868. The railroad first passed through Princeton on the south side of the canal, but in 1867 the route was straightened and thus Princeton Junction came into being. The shuttle train began running and despite changes in appearance has been in operation ever since. Apparently there was a shortage of rolling stock at first, for these cars came from the Belvidere Delaware Railroad Company. The old athletic field is in the background.

WEST CAMPUS, 1872. Westward expansion of the campus was marked by the erection of the Bonner Gymnasium and the Halsted Observatory. Cornerstone of the latter was laid in 1867. When completed, the Observatory consisted of an octagonal building flanked by two smaller wings. In the foreground is the railroad station on Railroad Avenue, as the new street was proudly named. In the background are the houses on Nassau Street.

WEST CAMPUS, 1879. By 1879 a new railroad station had appeared, as well as new houses on Railroad Avenue, soon to be renamed University Place. The most important of the new buildings on the west campus was Witherspoon Hall, completed in 1877. This dormitory, then considered an outstanding example of Victorian Gothic, was the most aristocratic, according to the undergraduates who eagerly sought to get rooms there from the departing seniors.

REUNION HALL. Reunion Hall was built in 1870 and was so named to commemorate the reunion of the Old and New Schools of the Presbyterian Church. It was located on the former site of the Joseph Henry House, which was then moved across the campus to the present site of the Chapel. This view was made in 1881. In modern times the two lower floors of this dormitory have been used for college offices and for various student publications.

THE DEAN'S HOUSE. Known as the President's House between 1756 and 1878, and subsequently called the Dean's House, this delightful colonial structure has witnessed the passing traffic on Nassau Street for two centuries. It had the same architect, Robert Smith, as Nassau Hall. A front porch and the eastern bay window were added in 1868, while the two ancient sycamores in front were planted in 1765. This view was taken in 1882.

PROFESSOR GUYOT'S GARDEN. The west campus was gradually developed by the acquisition of houses and lots along Nassau Street. Arnold Guyot's house and garden were on the present site of Holder Hall, and this view of his garden looks to the south where Campbell and Blair Halls are now located. Guyot's garden was justly famous for its rare plants, but the tradition that the weeping willows came from St. Helena was false.

UNIVERSITY HALL. Originally called the University Hotel, this structure was erected on the corner of Railroad Avenue (University Place) and Nassau Street in 1875. It was owned by a private corporation controlled by William Libbey, Sr.; but as a hotel it proved a white elephant. It subsequently was given over to use of the College and became a dormitory, but in 1916 it was demolished to make way for the new dining halls, collectively known as Madison Hall.

EDWARDS HALL. Edwards Hall was built in 1880 as a "poor man's dormitory," designed to accommodate those who could not afford to live in the elegant Witherspoon. It was of course named after the great theologian.

DICKINSON HALL was constructed as a classroom building in 1870. Of Romanesque appearance, it was soon remodeled to conform with the prevailing taste for Victorian Gothic. Dickinson became famous not only for the grim Examination Room under its eaves, but also for the class rushes which took place in front of the main doorway. It lasted for fifty years, being burned in 1920 in the fire that removed both Dickinson and the Marquand Chapel.

CLOACA MAXIMA, in 1873. None of the early dormitories had toilets, campus outhouses being in universal use. A favorite sport was to set fire to the flimsy shacks, even at the cost of personal deprivation. In despair, the trustees hit upon a stone and brick solution to the vexing problem, and placed it between Whig and Clio, a little to the rear. Admittedly it couldn't be burned; but on aesthetic grounds it was soon filled in, to be succeeded by the "Crystal Palace."

CHANCELLOR GREEN LIBRARY. Trustees and faculty were so proud of this example of Victorian Gothic, erected in 1873, that they put it on the site of Philosophical Hall which had stood for seventy years as the counterpart to Stanhope. President McCosh wrote that "it is so situated as to make North College and Dickinson Hall appear the wings of it." The Library was named after Chancellor Henry W. Green 1820, and was given by his brother.

INTERIOR OF CHANCELLOR GREEN LIBRARY. Not many books had been moved into Chancellor Green by 1874, but the modern undergraduate would recognize the place. Its stained glass and inadequate lighting continued a menace to good eyesight for over seventy years. Chancellor Green was the fourth repository of the College's library; books were originally kept in a second-floor room in Nassau Hall, then in Stanhope, and then in the Faculty Room.

THE OLD CANNON. A view in 1893 looking toward the Old Chapel, Chancellor Green and the west end of Dickinson. This Cannon, the bigger of two left here after the Battle of Princeton, was removed to New Brunswick in the War of 1812. It remained there until 1835 when sixteen members of the Princeton Blues brought it back as far as Queenston. Then in 1838 an expedition organized by Leonard W. Jerome brought it as far as the campus. For two years it lay prone, a challenge to any strong man. It was subsequently sunk, muzzle down, back of Nassau Hall, where it has been the center of cannon rushes, class day activities, and championship bonfires. It was the small Cannon, sunk between the Halls, which was carried off by Rutgers students in 1875 and was later returned, after an era of ill feeling.

BULLETIN ELM. The ancient elm between the Old Chapel and East College acquired its name because on it students tacked signs of furniture sales, class proclamations, and what not. This view, in 1871, apparently was taken at a time when activities were slack.

THE SCHOOL OF SCIENCE. The John C. Green School of Science Building was completed in 1874, being erected on the north-east corner of the campus. It contained classrooms, lecture halls, and laboratories. In the twentieth century it came to be regarded as an architectural monstrosity, and few mourned its destruction by fire in 1928. On the right is Dickinson Hall.

The School of Science Building was named in honor of its donor, John C. Green, wealthy New York merchant.

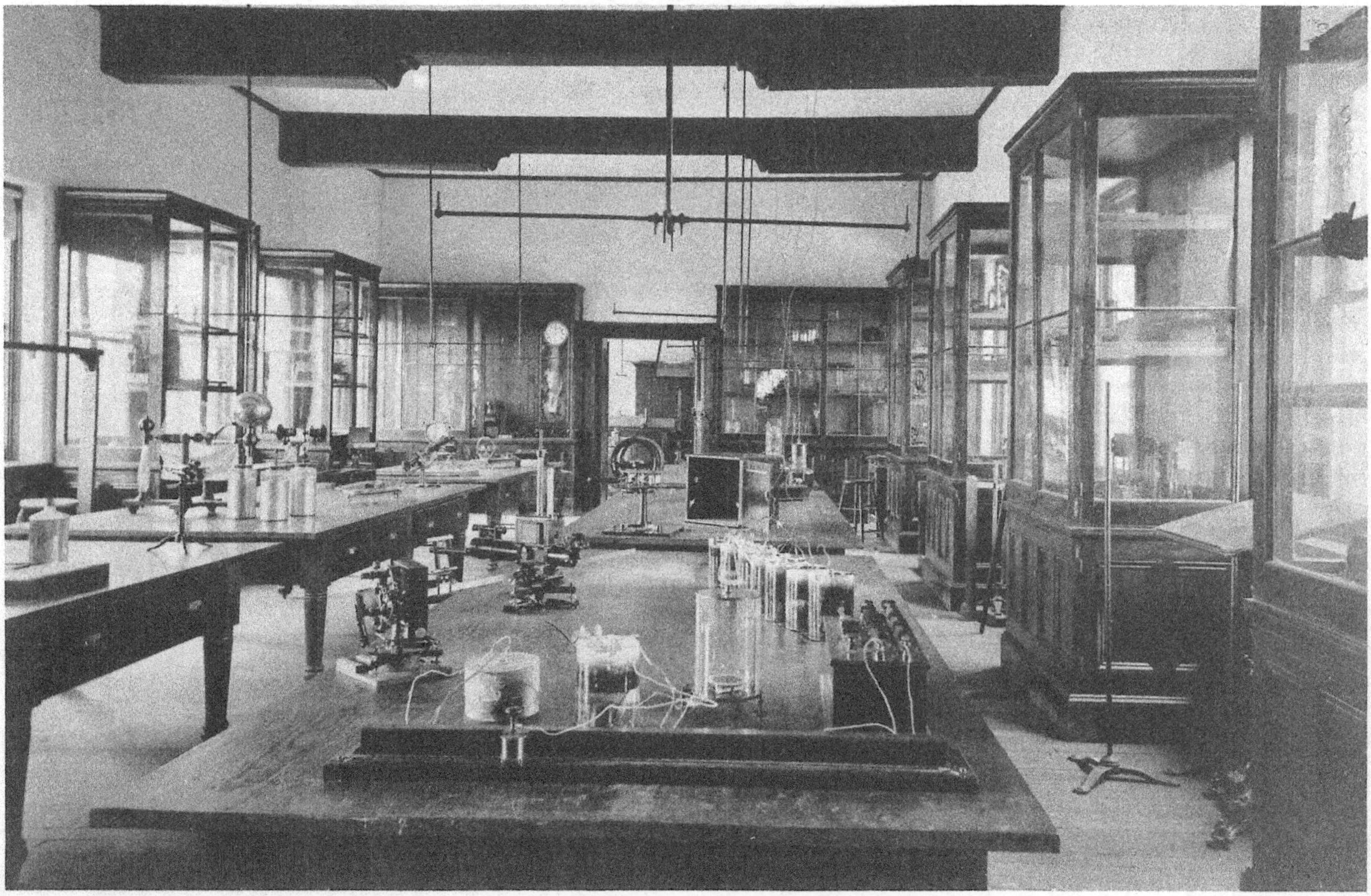

SCHOOL OF SCIENCE BUILDING, INTERIOR. View of the electrical laboratory in 1881. The numerous gifts of the Green family were used not only for buildings but also for endowment, new professorships being created.

PROSPECT AND PRESIDENT McCOSH, 1883. Prospect was purchased for the use of the President in 1878. It took its name from an earlier house on the same site owned by Col. George Morgan, famous Indian agent. Prospect was built in 1849 by the Potter family. This view shows the purple wisteria in an early stage; it now covers the south side of Prospect.

Prospect's Gardens slope to the south and constitute one of the beauty spots of the campus. A few trees originally set out by Col. Morgan are still flourishing. The alumni are entertained in the Gardens at each Reunion.

ORIGINAL McCOSH WALK. The east side of the campus originally had a grove of pine trees. A path through them later became known as McCosh Walk.

McCOSH WALK. The President, for whom the Walk was named, is here pictured on his favorite route. The early pines have now been replaced by elms.

President McCosh delighted in laying out new paths and in selecting the sites for new buildings, and it was under his administration that the College departed from the symmetry and balance that had earlier obtained on the campus. Slowly the landscaping at Princeton assumed the appearance of an English park, McCosh himself commenting that it was done "somewhat on the model of the demesnes of English gentlemen."

Mrs. McCosh likewise took an interest in the campus landscaping, and to the old elms and maples she added decorative blooming trees and shrubs, planting them at strategic points.

ROSE AND SON

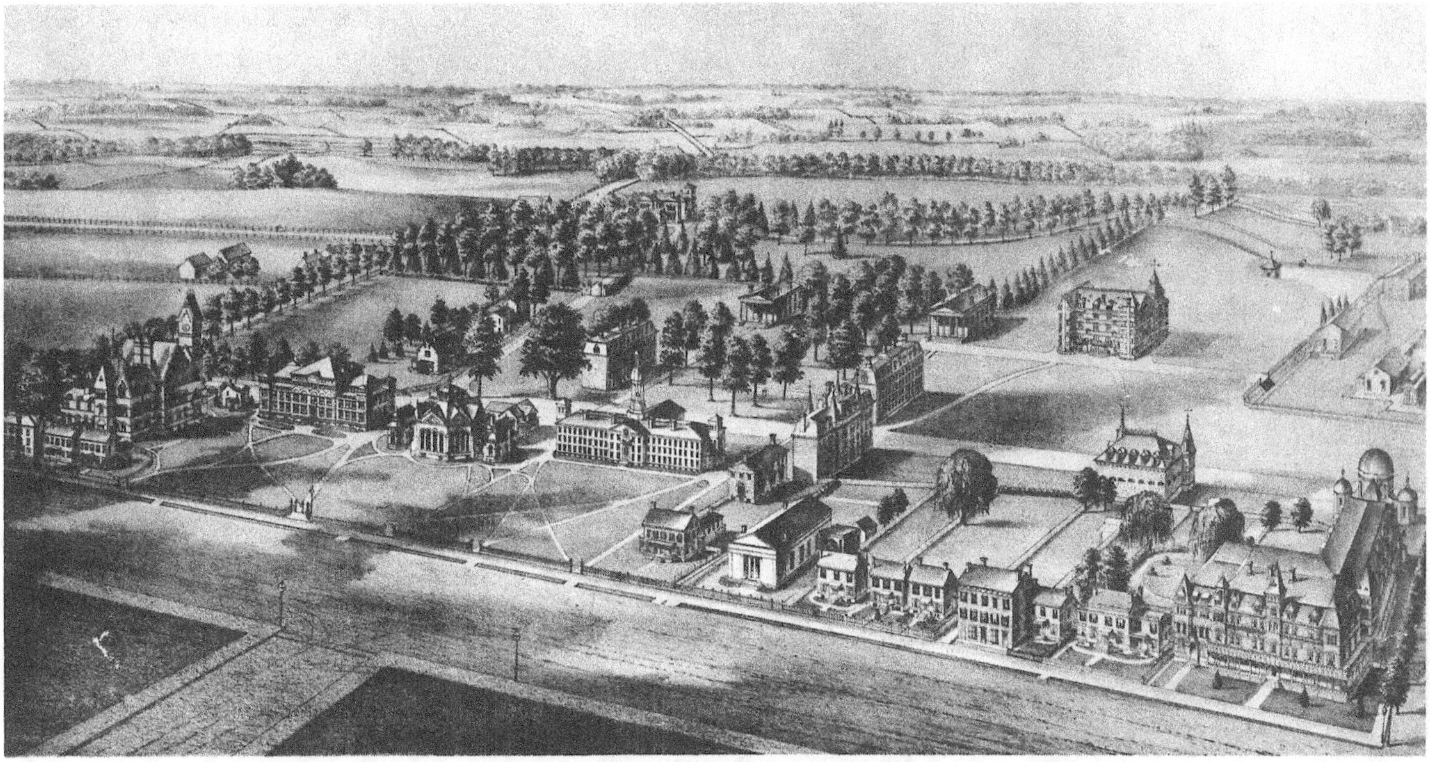

THE PRINCETON CAMPUS IN 1877. A birdseye view of the campus, from a lithograph published in 1875 by C. O. Hudnut of Princeton. The lithograph anticipated the building of Witherspoon Hall by two years; it is here designated as a New Dormitory. For the sake of clarity, many trees were omitted in this view.

NASSAU STREET AND THE FRONT CAMPUS, 1874. This picture was apparently taken at high noon, but hardly a soul was stirring. In the nineteenth century Nassau Street was nothing more than the main street of a country village.

MARQUAND CHAPEL. The Old Chapel was soon outgrown after the Civil War, when the number of undergraduates doubled. Marquand Chapel, the gift of Henry G. Marquand, was dedicated in 1882; it was built close to the site of the present Chapel. It burned in 1920 at the same time as Dickinson Hall.

CHAPEL INTERIOR. Marquand Chapel was designed by Richard M. Hunt and was constructed in the form of a Greek cross. Its interior was decorated with frescoes and stained glass.

THE EAST CAMPUS. The Joseph Henry House was moved to the east campus in 1870. This view, in the 1880's, shows the new Marquand Chapel as well as the drinking fountain which stood on the site of the Pyne Library.

FRONT CAMPUS LIFE, IN 1888. In warm weather students often lolled on the front campus, sometimes using the settees provided for that purpose. The close observer will note the Lions, not the Tigers, on the Steps.

OBSERVATORY OF INSTRUCTION. The working Observatory, on Prospect Avenue, was built in 1878. The house was long occupied by Professor Charles A. Young, famous astronomer. The Observatory and house are still in use, containing the departmental library and offices.

CLASS OF 1877 LABORATORY. The decennial gift of the Class of 1877, this structure was used as a biological laboratory until the building of Guyot freed it for other purposes. It survived until 1946 when the new Library necessitated its demolition.

MUSEUM OF HISTORIC ART. This view was taken soon after its dedication. Begun in 1887 it was originally designed as part of a larger building; the Museum has been remodeled but never completed. Instead, McCormick Hall was added on the west side in the 1920's.

Alumni of the Middle Period

IT IS RATHER AN ASTONISHING FACT that the alumni graduated during the period of Princeton's decline attained positions of leadership only less important than in the previous period. It is true of course that in politics Princeton had no figures comparable to the earlier Burr and Madison, nor to the contemporary Daniel Webster of Dartmouth or John C. Calhoun of Yale. In letters she produced no alumni comparable to the New England group which was graduated from Harvard and Bowdoin. Yet of the 356 alumni who left Nassau Hall during the short administration of Ashbel Green, a decade marking the nadir of Princeton's history, twenty became college presidents; four, United States Senators; and eleven, Congressmen.

The growth of the alumni body following 1830 implied no diminution in the quality of leadership. The Civil War was evidence of that when Princeton furnished large numbers of officers to both sides, including eight general officers in the Confederate armies. In the postwar period, the Class of 1879 has generally been recognized as outstanding.

The nineteen alumni whose portraits are reproduced herewith have been selected rather arbitrarily, even more so than in the early period. They include four statesmen, two military figures, three ministers, two educators, one doctor, three men of letters, and four businessmen.

UNDERWOOD-STRATTON

WOODROW WILSON 1879. Princeton's greatest alumnus of modern times, Woodrow Wilson has by now assumed an almost settled position in history. One of the most controversial of figures, he inspired a devoted following and also aroused a bitter opposition. Of him President Seymour of Yale has written, "But just as it is certain that the nations will pursue the hope of establishing an international organization for the guarantee of peace, so it is certain that Wilson will remain historically the eminent prophet of that better world." (This photograph of Wilson was taken when he was Governor of New Jersey and living at 25 Cleveland Lane in Princeton, whence he commuted to the state Capitol.)

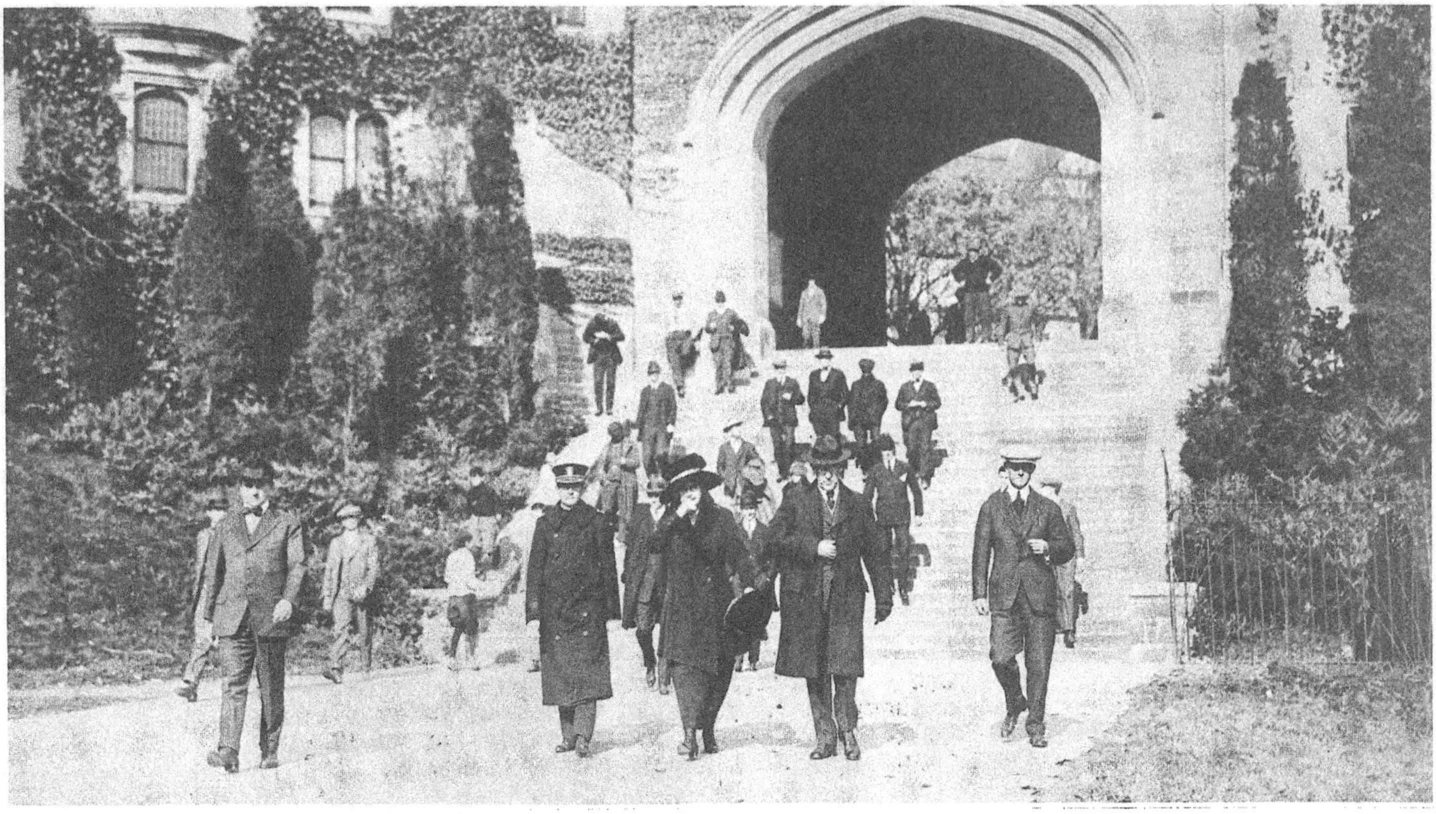

UNDERWOOD-STRATTON

As President of the United States, Woodrow Wilson was an occasional visitor in Princeton, especially on election days. Flanked by secret service operatives, the presidential party comes down the steps from Blair arch, in the fall of 1917. Accompanying Mr. and Mrs. Wilson is Rear Admiral Cary T. Grayson, U.S.N., aide to the President.

DEPARTMENT OF JUSTICE

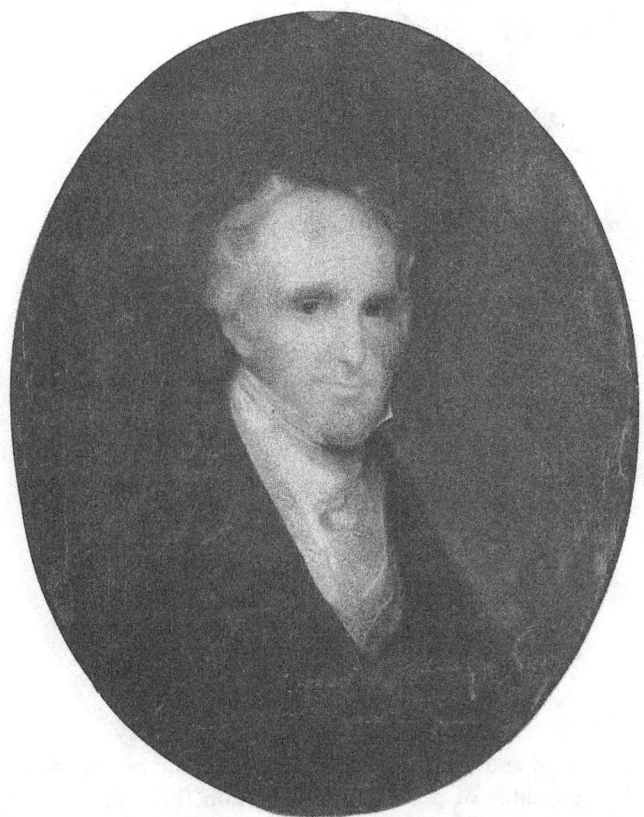

Richard Rush 1797. His versatile talents enabled him to serve as Attorney-General, Secretary of State, Secretary of the Treasury, and minister to England.

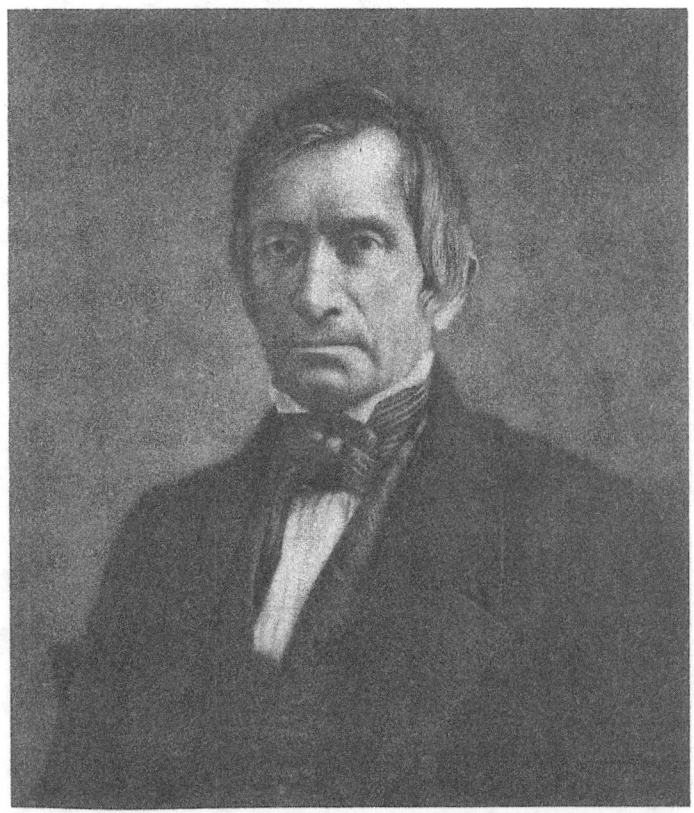

Theodore Frelinghuysen 1804. Of the distinguished New Jersey family, he served as United States Senator, Mayor of Newark, and for ten years as President of Rutgers.

THE HISTORICAL SOCIETY OF PENNSYLVANIA

GEORGE M. DALLAS 1810; from the portrait by J. Augustus Beck. Princeton's "other Vice President," he defeated Theodore Frelinghuysen 1804 in the election of 1844.

ROBERT F. STOCKTON 1813; from the Princeton portrait by Thomas Sully. Leaving Princeton for the Navy, he saw service in two wars and helped conquer California.

FRANCIS P. BLAIR, JR., 1841. Successively a Democrat, a Free Soiler, a Republican, and then a Democrat in his turbulent career, he saved Missouri for the Union.

CHARLES HODGE 1815. The leading Presbyterian theologian of the nineteenth century, he taught at the Theological Seminary and founded the *Princeton Review*.

JAMES C. HEPBURN 1832. The first medical missionary to Japan, he translated the Bible into Japanese and compiled a monumental Japanese-English dictionary.

KENYON COLLEGE

CHARLES P. MCILVAINE 1816. He became Episcopal Bishop of Ohio and President of Kenyon College. In the Civil War he lectured in England on the immorality of slavery.

HENRY FAIRFIELD OSBORN 1877. Able paleontologist, administrator, and author, he left Princeton to become head of the American Museum of Natural History.

LIVINGSTON FARRAND 1888. Scientist, relief worker, and educator, he became President of Cornell after serving with the International Health Board and the Red Cross.

THE HISTORICAL SOCIETY OF PENNSYLVANIA

GEORGE H. BOKER 1842; from a portrait as an undergraduate. A successful diplomat, poet, and playwright, he won great fame with his tragedies both here and abroad.

JOHN M. T. FINNEY 1884. A great surgeon at the Johns Hopkins, he developed several operations. To remain in his profession, he refused the presidency of Princeton.

N. BOOTH TARKINGTON 1893. The creator of Penrod, Alice Adams, and a host of other characters, "Old Tark," as his friends called him, endeared himself to all America.

HENRY VAN DYKE 1873. Author, educator, and diplomat, he left the ministry to teach at Princeton. He knew personally many of the English poets about whom he lectured.

NICHOLAS BIDDLE 1801. Although remembered today as a banker, Biddle had equal ability as a scholar and as a diplomat. His great duel with Jackson was his undoing.

LEONARD W. JEROME 1840. The grandfather of Winston Churchill brought the big Cannon to Princeton. But more important, he later controlled the *New York Times*.

CHARLES SCRIBNER 1840. He was the first of three generations to bear that name and direct the fortunes of one of America's most distinguished publishing firms.

MOSES TAYLOR PYNE 1877. A lawyer, banker, and railroad president, he was for many years regarded by Princetonians as the University's leading alumnus and benefactor.

The Recent Period 1888-1947

THE RECENT PERIOD covers that half century during which Princeton has existed as a university, although, as indicated above, the opening of that era has technically been placed at the accession of Francis L. Patton as President. Actually the transformation of Princeton from a small liberal arts college into a true university had already taken place under James McCosh. McCosh himself had urged the trustees to adopt the new name.

It remained for the formal change to be made at the sesquicentennial anniversary of Princeton in 1896. The old College of New Jersey legally became Princeton University, and a new seal was adopted. The celebration was marked by the presence of distinguished delegates from universities both here and abroad. Of the many speeches made, the most notable was by Professor Woodrow Wilson, whose widely-quoted *Princeton in the Nation's Service* brought him sharply to the attention of all.

President Patton's administration ended in 1902. Never a forceful leader, he permitted the new University to drift. He had a natural preference for private study and writing over wielding direct control over the University's expanding affairs. Many of the leading faculty members chafed at the administrative inactivity, and in part compensated for the lack of direction at the top. It was Professor Andrew F. West, for example, who was largely instrumental in settling the University's building policy in favor of English Gothic. For years the trustees had experimented with various architectural types, *vide* Witherspoon, Dod and Brown Halls. But beginning with Blair Hall in 1897, Princeton turned definitely to Oxford for architectural inspiration and has remained consistent in that policy ever since.

The election of Woodrow Wilson as President meant the end of Princeton's period of "expansion and inaction." The building program, under Wilson, was accompanied by an even more remarkable raising of academic standards. The curriculum was revised and a framework of departments and divisions established; no longer could an undergraduate wander aimlessly in a forest of almost free electives. With Henry B. Fine as Dean of the Faculty, the new administration called many young men of talent to Princeton.

In 1905 came the introduction of the preceptorial system, inspired by the tutorial system that had existed at Oxford and Cambridge for centuries. The preceptorial, which has since been one of the cherished features of Princeton education, was largely the innovation of Wilson, but it is fair to state that the preceptorial plan as was first envisaged has since been modified. Originally the preceptors were regarded as a temporary body in the faculty, to be constantly renewed and replaced. The first group of preceptors who arrived in 1905 proved such able scholars and teachers, however, that not to keep them permanently would have been disastrous. Out of this original group came many of the great scholars and administrators of a later period.

The last three years of Wilson's administration were marked by a lack of harmony which contrasted with the co-operation and achievements of the first five. His attempts to introduce a "quadrangle plan," by which the upperclass eating clubs might be integrated with "colleges" of the University, met defeat. Of greater importance was the struggle between Wilson and Dean West over the location and control of the Graduate College. The two had long worked together, and the rift first appeared over the "quadrangle plan." Whereas Wilson wanted the Graduate College to be on the campus to promote intellectual and social contacts, Dean West and certain trustees favored a site further removed. When substantial donors favored the latter, a majority of the trustees were won over and Wilson yielded. His resignation in 1910, to enter politics, closed an administration in which Princeton had made great strides.

The accession of John G. Hibben to the presidency meant an end to dissension within the Princeton family. Representing no faction "but one united Princeton," Dr. Hibben was instrumental in healing the split between the West and Wilson groups. His administration, despite the interruption of World War I, directed a vast expansion of the Princeton campus. The prosperous 'twenties saw the southwestern section become covered with new Gothic dormitories; while on the east side, new laboratories, classroom buildings, and finally the great Chapel appeared, the last standing almost as a personal monument to Hibben. Nor were all gifts invested in stone and brick. Endowment funds were steadily increased, and faculty salaries raised. Undergraduate standards were heightened by the inauguration of the four-course plan. When Hibben retired in 1932, he could look back upon two decades of remarkable progress, an era in which the endowment had quintupled and the student enrollment had increased by over a thousand.

Under the presidency of Harold W. Dodds, Princeton successfully met the manifold problems imposed by the depression, World War II, and the post-war influx of students; in addition, the University continued with its program of self-analysis and improvement. The building program concentrated on Library and Gymnasium. For undergraduates a New Plan of Study was devised by which a divisional grouping of courses underlies the specialization of senior year, the purpose being to develop the critical, analytical, and creative powers of the student. As Princeton celebrated its bicentennial anniversary in 1946-1947, its vision was more on the future than on the past, distinguished and satisfying as that had been.

The Presidents

FRANCIS LANDEY PATTON 1888-1902

FRANCIS LANDEY PATTON, professor of ethics in the College and also a member of the faculty of the Theological Seminary, succeeded McCosh as President. His selection was disappointing to many alumni who would have preferred a Princeton graduate, but Patton soon overcame this prejudice and won the general liking of both alumni and undergraduates. He was a witty and brilliant speaker, and he gradually transformed his severe clerical appearance. Eventually "the more secular black tie supplanted the white tie for business wear. The austere whiskers were shorn away." He even took an interest in athletics, vigorously applauding when a touchdown was made.

Under his administration physical expansion carried on apace, several new dormitories, Alexander Hall, and the Pyne Library being constructed. The outstanding event of his administration was, of course, the sesquicentennial anniversary in 1896 when the College of New Jersey became Princeton University.

In 1902 Patton resigned the presidency. His main fault as administrator was that he did not provide the leadership necessary to a university that was rapidly growing.

(From the portrait by John W. Alexander in the Faculty Room.)

WOODROW WILSON 1879 was the first President who was not a clergyman, but as a minister's son he satisfied those who disliked too sharp a break with tradition. A distinguished political scientist and historian, and a popular teacher, Wilson had definite ideas about education and the course that he wanted Princeton to take.

His radical revision of the curriculum and the introduction of the preceptorial system constituted the two great achievements of his administration. It is significant that it was the younger faculty members, especially the preceptors, who gave him their united support in the controversies over the "quadrangle plan" and the Graduate College. Probably Wilson was unnecessarily insistent that the College be located in the heart of the campus; and it was unfortunate that his brilliant administration should end with a certain amount of dissension.

His decision to enter politics was not a sudden one but was made only after several years of consideration. He resigned after being nominated for the governorship of New Jersey.

(From the portrait by Frederick B. Yates in Whig Hall.)

WOODROW WILSON 1902-1910

JOHN GRIER HIBBEN 1912-1932

JOHN GRIER HIBBEN 1882 became President after the short interregnum in which Dean Fine carried on the administrative duties. "A loyal Princetonian, through and through," Hibben was the ideal choice to restore harmony to alumni and faculty. The valedictorian of his class, he had gone through the Theological Seminary, entered the Princeton faculty, and had become a popular teacher of philosophy and the Bible. He had won an international reputation for his writings, of which perhaps *The Philosophy of the Enlightenment* was the best known.

Under Hibben's administration, Princeton experienced an enormous growth in which both the undergraduate body and the faculty doubled in size. The scientific departments were especially benefitted, and there were inaugurated the School of Architecture, the School of Engineering, and the School of Public and International Affairs.

Despite Princeton's vast increase in size, President Hibben remained the head of a great household. Mrs. Hibben, like Mrs. McCosh, always took a personal interest in the students, often visiting them in the Infirmary; while Prospect was thrown open to them on Christmas Eve.

A firm believer in academic freedom, Hibben won the united support of the faculty. The four-course plan, introduced in 1923, provided for independent reading and a thesis by upperclassmen; for most students the individual work now required proved a rewarding intellectual adventure.

(From the portrait by Julian Lamar in the Faculty Room.)

HAROLD WILLIS DODDS became President in 1933, following a one-year interval in which Edward D. Duffield 1892 served as Acting President following Dr. Hibben's retirement.

With the exception of Aaron Burr, Dr. Dodds was the youngest President to assume office, yet none had had wider experience in the practical world of affairs. After graduation from Grove City College and advanced study at Princeton and the University of Pennsylvania, he gained an international reputation as an expert in municipal government and the conduct of elections. He was for thirteen years editor of *The National Municipal Review*.

For his work in Latin America Dr. Dodds received wide acclaim. He twice served as electoral adviser in Nicaragua, was technical adviser to the Tacna-Arica Plebiscitary Commission, and acted as arbiter in an election dispute in Cuba.

At Princeton, where he joined the faculty in 1925, he fully demonstrated his great administrative abilities. The School of Public and International Affairs and the Princeton Surveys developed under his watchful attention. President Dodds's administration of the University has been marked by an increased endowment and a building program closely fitted to the University's needs. The new Firestone Library and the Dillon Gymnasium will stand as monuments to his administration. Historians will note it furthermore as a period in which the difficulties attendant upon World War II were met and conquered.

(From the portrait by Ellen E. Rand in the Faculty Room.)

HAROLD WILLIS DODDS 1933–

Administration and Faculty

SAMUEL R. WINANS 1874 was the second Dean of the Faculty, succeeding Dean Murray in 1899. A professor of Greek and an instructor in Sanskrit, he was an enthusiastic expounder of Greek civilization to the undergraduates. One of his pupils has recorded that "intellectual elegance" best expresses the spirit of his teaching.

HENRY B. FINE 1880 became Dean of the Faculty under Wilson in 1903, and the two worked closely together in raising academic standards. Himself a distinguished mathematician, he had an uncanny faculty for recognizing talent in young scientists. He administered the University between 1910 and 1912, and then continued to hold the special position of Dean of the Departments of Science until his death.

WILLIAM F. MAGIE 1879 was the valedictorian of his famous class. For twenty years the chairman of the Physics Department, he succeeded Dean Fine as Dean of the Faculty in 1912. His interests in science were broad and in World War I he carried out experiments in the development of camouflage. He was a founder of the American Physical Society.

SAMUEL ROSS WINANS

HENRY BURCHARD FINE

WILLIAM FRANCIS MAGIE

ORREN JACK TURNER

RICHARD CARVER WOOD
LUTHER PFAHLER EISENHART

CLEAROSE STUDIO
ROBERT KILBURN ROOT

LUTHER P. EISENHART, leading mathematician and administrator, is the only faculty member to have been both Dean of the Faculty and Dean of the Graduate School. He succeeded Dean Magie in 1925 and promoted the four-course plan; eight years later he moved to the Wyman House. He retired in 1945. His educational philosophy is best expressed in his recent volume, *The Educational Process*.

ROBERT K. ROOT came to Princeton from Yale as one of the original "preceptor guys" in 1905. His courses in English, including the one familiarly known as "Root's Roots," were famous for the polished brilliance of his lectures, while in the world of scholarship he became known as an outstanding authority on Chaucer and Pope. He became Dean of the Faculty in 1933, retiring with the rearguard of the preceptors in 1946.

J. DOUGLAS BROWN 1919, professor of economics and Director of the Industrial Relations Section, succeeded Dean Root as Dean of the Faculty in 1946. Frequently called as a consultant, he helped plan the Social Security Act of 1935 and in World War II assisted the Secretary of War in vital problems of manpower and training.

JAMES DOUGLAS BROWN

Emerson's adage about an institution being the lengthened shadow of a man was never better exemplified than in the life of Dean ANDREW FLEMING WEST 1874. Princeton's Graduate School was almost solely his creation; for it he worked indefatigably, and sometimes he had to fight. He was its Dean for twenty-seven years, until his retirement in 1928.

His controversy with President Wilson over the location and control of the Graduate College became historic. The outcome of that struggle constituted one of the "if's" of history, for it led Wilson to leave academic life and to enter politics. A tireless campaigner for endowment, Dean West approached Isaac C. Wyman 1846, elderly bachelor of Salem, who had willed his money to Harvard. When the usual arguments failed, West closed the conversation by asking quietly, "Where did your father fight—in the Battle of Cambridge or the Battle of Princeton?" Wyman's father as a boy of seventeen had fought under Washington at Princeton; and the Wyman bequest ended the struggle between West and Wilson.

Perhaps too much significance has been accorded to the controversy. The two men, with President Eliot of Harvard, were the outstanding educational leaders in the country; and, in their time, the two were most instrumental in furthering Princeton as a university.

Dean West will long be remembered by graduate students for the interest he took in their research, and for his charm and endless fund of anecdotes in conversation. Faculty members remember him best as a stalwart champion of the classics in the Faculty Room, and as the author of those famous presentations for honorary degrees, noble classics of English prose.

ANDREW FLEMING WEST

AUGUSTUS TROWBRIDGE succeeded Dean West as head of the Graduate School and held this position for five years. A brilliant physicist, in World War I he developed flash-and-sound-ranging devices to orient hostile batteries, the mechanical phases of this task being carried out in Palmer Physical Laboratory. After the war, he served in the International Education Board as director of science for Europe. A strict and stimulating teacher, he was also a capable administrator who won the admiration of graduate students after the retirement of Dean West.

ORREN JACK TURNER

AUGUSTUS TROWBRIDGE

HUGH S. TAYLOR became the fourth Dean of the Graduate School in 1945, succeeding Dean Eisenhart. Chairman of the Department of Chemistry since 1926, he played a prominent part in the mobilization of science for war purposes. His personal research included the discovery of the most effective catalyst for producing heavy water in connection with the atomic bomb program.

EDWARD G. ELLIOTT 1897 was the first Dean of the College, that office being created in 1909 to handle matters of discipline. A popular professor in the Department of History, Politics, and Economics, he produced five scholarly works. He left the University in 1912 to live in California, and has in recent years been engaged in banking.

HOWARD McCLENAHAN 1895 was Dean of the College between 1912 and 1925, when he resigned to become secretary of the Franklin Institute of Philadelphia. An exacting but witty teacher of physics, "Dean Mac" was one of the most popular faculty members of his period. Under his leadership as chairman of the Board of Athletic Control, Princeton set and maintained strict standards of athletic eligibility.

HUGH STOTT TAYLOR

EDWARD GRAHAM ELLIOTT

HOWARD McCLENAHAN

ROSE AND SON

For twenty years Dean of the College, CHRISTIAN GAUSS had come to Princeton as one of the original preceptors. When he retired in 1945, he was promptly made honorary Dean of the Alumni. Long chairman of the Department of Modern Languages and a scholar of note, Dean Gauss had an enormous influence on his students, best evidenced in the fact that some forty former pupils have dedicated books to him.

FRANCIS R. B. GODOLPHIN 1924, professor of classics, returned from World War II and succeeded Christian Gauss as Dean of the College. As an officer of the Marine Corps he stormed ashore with the landing waves at Kwajalein, Tinian, Saipan, and Luzon. As Dean he has efficiently met the problems imposed by the vast post-war influx of G.I.'s.

ARTHUR M. GREENE, JR., became the first Dean of the School of Engineering in 1921, and retired in 1940. A professor of mechanical engineering and the author of many standard works, he is held in affectionate regard today by many of his former students. Besides his active association with professional societies, he has often served as consultant.

BACHRACH
CHRISTIAN GAUSS

FRANCIS RICHARD BORROUM GODOLPHIN

RICHARD CARVER WOOD
ARTHUR MAURICE GREENE, JR.

KENNETH HAMILTON CONDIT
BACHRACH

RADCLIFFE HEERMANCE

KENNETH H. CONDIT 1913 was called back to Princeton in 1940 to succeed Dean Greene. After his graduation from Princeton he had entered the faculty, and in 1917 had helped organize the Princeton School of Military Aeronautics. After serving with distinction in World War I, he became editor of the *American Machinist* and *Product Engineering*. In World War II he organized research projects at Princeton.

RADCLIFFE HEERMANCE, Director of Admission, is held in especial regard by Princeton men of the present generation, for he has picked the personnel of the incoming classes since 1921. He has also been, for varying intervals, Dean of the Freshmen and Acting Dean of the College. Known as the "Genial Dean," he was long one of the most popular lecturers and preceptors of the English Department.

ROBERT R. WICKS became Dean of the University Chapel in 1928, the first incumbent of that office which was established upon the completion of the Chapel. His sermons were very popular with undergraduates and the numerous visitors whom he attracted. The Dean's philosophy has been further expounded in *The Reason for Living*. He retired in 1947.

RICHARD CARVER WOOD
ROBERT RUSSELL WICKS

Two Geology Expeditions. The eminence in geology which Arnold H. Guyot gave Princeton was greatly enhanced by the work of WILLIAM B. SCOTT 1877, who succeeded Guyot as Blair professor of geology. Scott led a long series of western expeditions in which important discoveries of fossils were made.

In the upper picture is the expedition of 1886, in northern Utah: from left to right sitting on the ground are Jake Heisey who acted as guide; Nicholas M. Butler, then a tutor at Columbia; David E. Harlan 1886; Francis Speir, Jr., 1877; Francis F. Kane 1886; and Walter E. Harvey 1886. Behind are Stewart Paton 1886; William Powell; and Joseph D. Baucus 1886.

In the center picture of the expedition of 1891 in Montana, are, standing: William F. Magie 1879; Cyrus Jefferson; and Charlie, the cook. Kneeling are Professor Scott; and Robert A. Stevenson 1892. And reposing are Richard Coulter 1892; James F. Hosford 1892; Arthur W. Butler 1892; and George, the teamster.

Expedition at Home. Excavation for the new Firestone Library in 1946 revealed that the eastern section of the campus, some twenty feet down, had been the bottom of a lake 175 million years ago. Here Professor Glenn L. Jepsen 1927 collects fossils of ancient lungfish while a few undergraduates watch the operation.

HOWARD CROSBY BUTLER

In the world of scholarship probably nothing better proved Princeton's claim to the name of University than the work done in Near Eastern archaeology. The guiding spirit was Professor HOWARD CROSBY BUTLER 1892, who led three expeditions to Syria and one to Sardis. He was assisted by such scholars as Professors William K. Prentice 1892, David Magie 1897, Enno Littmann, Eric Brunnow, and Mr. Robert Garrett 1897.

Professor T. Leslie Shear resumed the work at Sardis after World War I; he later directed the excavation of the Agora at Athens.

Here are two views, taken in 1913, of the excavations at Sardis, which reveal the huge Temple of Artemis.

Luncheon at Antioch, 1936. Excavations at Antioch and vicinity were carried out between 1932 and 1939 by an expedition conducted by Princeton, in which other institutions joined. The project was under the general supervision of the departmental chairman, Professor CHARLES R. MOREY, assisted by members of the Department of Art and Archaeology and other scholars.

At this informal luncheon, from left to right, are: Mlle. Maillart, a visitor; Charles R. Morey; Miss Gladys Baker, staff member; Miss Myrtilla Avery, of Wellesley; William A. Campbell, field director; Robert Garrett 1897; Francis H. Taylor, then director of the Worcester Art Museum; Richard Stillwell 1921; and W. H. Noble, staff member.

Faculty Baseball Squad, 1896. Baseball was the favorite campus sport in the nineteenth century. The academic and scientific departments of the faculty were consistent rivals on the diamond. Here are the faculty players in 1896, from left to right: Fred Neher 1889; Frederic C. Torrey; William Libbey 1877 (above); Willard Humphreys; B. Franklin Carter 1894; Jonathan B. Chittenden; William G. Howard; John M. Brooks 1889; Lewis S. Mudge 1889; Howard C. Warren 1889; William K. Prentice 1892; Charles H. Hinton; James P. Atkinson 1892; Charles S. Smith 1888; Williamson U. Vreeland 1892; Bliss Perry; Harry F. Covington 1892; and Herbert F. Sill 1894 (with mitt).

Presenting the Sun Dial. The Mather Sun Dial is a copy of the one erected at Corpus Christi College at Oxford in 1551. At the formal presentation ceremonies in 1907, President Wilson introduced Lord Bryce, the British Ambassador, who made the principal address.

By undergraduate custom, only seniors may sit on the steps below the Sun Dial.

The Bachelors Club. The house of the Bachelors Club stood for years at the foot of University Place; but when, in 1918, the new railroad station was built, the old frame structure had to be moved. The Club later occupied other quarters, and eventually found its last retreat in the safe confines of the Nassau Club, where its identity became lost in the general membership. The Bachelors Club was composed of young unmarried faculty members, with an occasional figure from administration or the University Press. This group picture, made in the spring of 1908, includes many of the preceptors whom Wilson called to Princeton.

From left to right, on the front step: La Rue Van Hook; Fred L. Hutson; Gilbert F. Close; Donald C. Stuart; and Samuel S. Feagles 1900.

On the second step: William Foster; Ralph B. Pomeroy; John G. Hun; and Herring Winship.

On the third step: Hardin Craig; Edward G. Spaulding; William H. Clemons; Charles F. Silvester; Henry R. Shipman; and Charles D. Mahaffie.

On the fourth step: Alfred E. Richards; Harvey W. Thayer; William S. Myers; and Philip H. Fogel.

On the fifth step: Sigmund G. Spaeth; Edwin M. Rankin (behind); Donald Cameron; Morris W. Croll; Charles H. McIlwain 1894; Francis C. MacDonald 1896; Andrew R. Anderson; Lionel H. Duschak; and Charles E. Mathews.

Standing on the left: Gordon H. Gerould; Wilmon H. Sheldon; and Oswald Veblen (behind).

Front row in chairs: Edward S. Corwin; H. Lester Cooke; Harold R. Hastings; George T. Northrup; Charles E. Lyon; and Raymond S. Dugan.

Second row in chairs: Charles R. MacInnes; George M. Galt; Harry B. Van Deventer; Nathaniel E. Griffin; John W. Basore; George D. Kellogg; and Henry B. Dewing.

Rear row, standing: Charles W. Kennedy; George W. T. Whitney; Walter L. Whittlesey; Ernest L. Bogart; and Philip E. Robinson 1898.

Presenting the Lake, 1906. Lake Carnegie was the gift of the famous steel manufacturer, who had a nostalgia for the lochs of his native Scotland. Ceremonies were held in Alexander Hall in December 1906, at which Andrew Carnegie formally presented deeds to the Lake Carnegie Association. Here President Wilson and Carnegie lead the academic procession, followed by trustees John A. Stewart, Moses T. Pyne 1877, and Cleveland H. Dodge 1879 (on right). Needless to say, the undergraduates were overjoyed at the prospect of aquatic sports; although Wilson, who had hoped for a more academic gift, later remarked, as one Scot-Irish to a Scot, "We asked for bread and you gave us cake."

PHOTO BY BROWN BROTHERS

ROSE AND SON

The English Department, 1910. The English Department has long been one of Princeton's outstanding departments. During Wilson's administration it was greatly strengthened by the addition of preceptors some of whom have only recently retired.

Front row, left to right: Herbert S. Murch; Francis C. MacDonald 1896; Morris W. Croll; Charles W. Kennedy; Radcliffe Heermance; and George D. Brown.

Second row: J. Duncan Spaeth; Robert K. Root; Gordon H. Gerould; Augustus W. Long; Hardin Craig; and L. Wardlaw Miles.

Third row: Stockton Axson; Thomas M. Parrott 1888; and George McL. Harper 1884. Standing: Nathaniel E. Griffin.

Top row: Henry van Dyke 1773 (in oval); Charles G. Osgood; Harry F. Covington 1892; Theodore W. Hunt 1865; and Harry W. Clemons.

President Hibben's Inauguration. Dr. Hibben's inauguration, in May 1912, was marked by the presence of President William H. Taft and Edward D. White, Chief Justice of the United States, as well as the heads of the leading eastern universities.

In the academic procession Dr. Hibben accompanies President Taft, while behind the latter is White. Associate Justice Mahlon Pitney 1879 administered the oath of office to Dr. Hibben.

PHOTO BY BROWN BROTHERS

President Hibben and Trustees. Until recently the trustees have been rarely photographed. This picture was taken about 1920. Practically all the family names are distinguished in Princeton history for two or more generations.

Front row, left to right: John O. H. Pitney 1881; Henry B. Thompson 1877; President John G. Hibben 1882; Moses T. Pyne 1877; and Parker D. Handy 1879.

Second row: Robert Garrett 1897; Charles Scribner 1875; William C. Procter 1883; Alexander Van Rensselaer 1871; and Melancthon W. Jacobus 1877.

Third row: John Stuart 1900; Matthew C. Fleming 1886; Bayard Henry 1876; and T. Williams Roberts 1899.

ORREN JACK TURNER

PHOTO BY BROWN BROTHERS

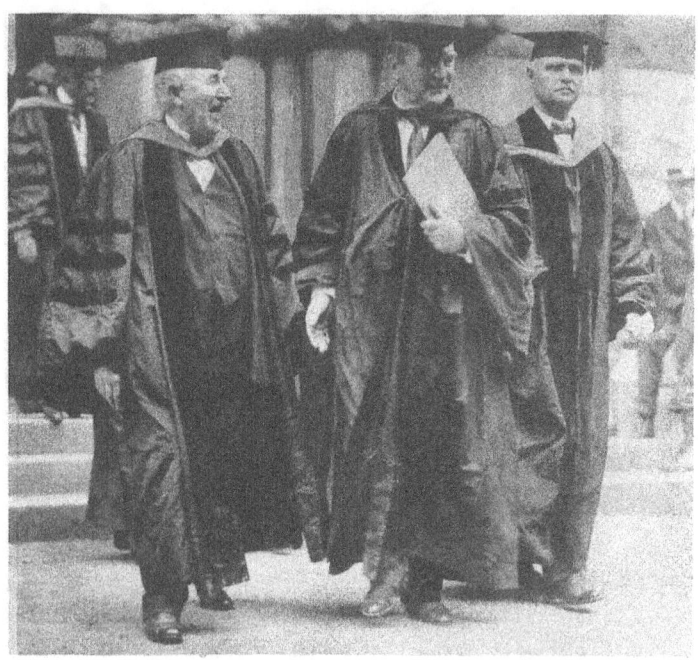

Dean West Makes a Point. No finer presentations for honorary degrees were ever composed by an American educator than those written by Dean Andrew Fleming West. The Dean's mastery of English prose was. to many, one of the most powerful arguments for study of the classics.

Two recipients of honorary degrees in 1915 stand with Dean West in front of Alexander Hall. On the left, Thomas A. Edison; and, on the right, General George W. Goethals.

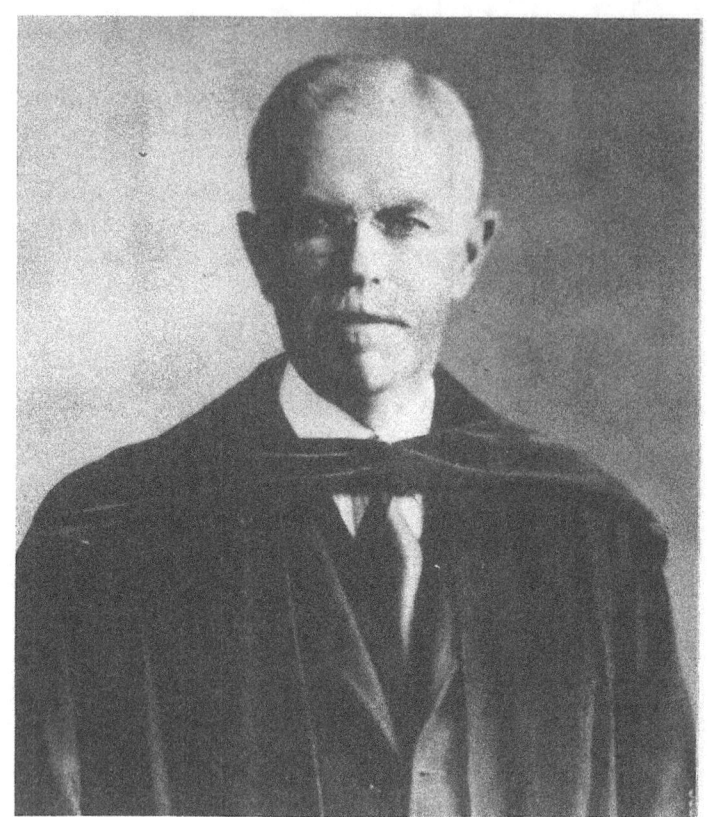

Portrait Study of President Hibben.

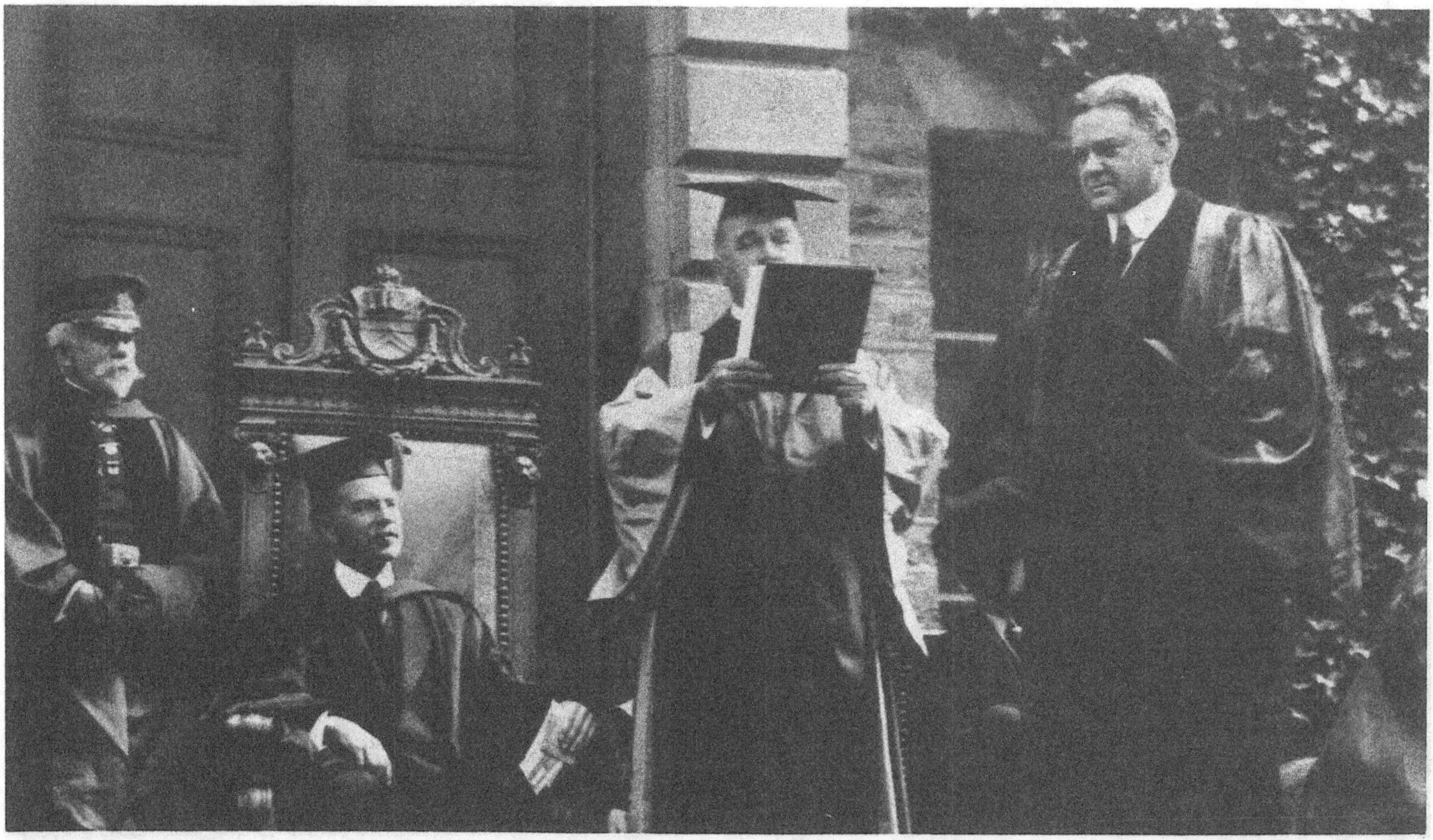

PHOTO BY BROWN BROTHERS

Honoris Causa. Dean West presenting Herbert Clark Hoover for the degree of Doctor of Laws at the commencement in 1917. President Hibben, and Professor William Libbey, then in wartime service, listen attentively.

University Administrative Officers, 1932. At the close of President Hibben's administration in 1932, this group picture was taken of the officers serving under him.

Front row, left to right: Varnum L. Collins 1892, Secretary; Dean Christian Gauss; Dean Andrew F. West 1874; President Hibben; Dean William F. Magie 1879; Dean Luther P. Eisenhart; George C. Wintringer 1894, Controller.

Second row: Dr. Joseph E. Raycroft; Henry G. Duffield 1881, Treasurer; Dean Radcliffe Heermance; Gordon G. Sikes 1916, Assistant to the Secretary; Dean Robert R. Wicks; and Dean Arthur M. Greene, Jr.

Third row: Edward A. MacMillan 1914, Superintendent of Grounds and Buildings; Asa S. Bushnell 1921, Graduate Manager of Athletics; Clifford D. Quick, Assistant to the Superintendent of Grounds and Buildings; and B. Franklin Bunn 1907, Manager of the University Store.

Fourth row: Gail A. Mills, Assistant Treasurer; George R. Meyers 1922, Assistant to the Superintendent of Grounds and Buildings; John S. Cosgrave, Assistant Treasurer; Wilbur F. Kerr, Registrar; Frederic E. Camp 1928, Assistant to the Dean of the College; Frederick S. Osborne 1924, Director of Public Information; and Ledlie I. Laughlin 1912, Assistant to the Director of Admission.

Fifth row: Dr. Willard G. Rainey; Robert G. Albion, Assistant Dean; Stephen F. Voorhees 1900, Supervising Architect; Thurston J. Davies 1916, Secretary of the Graduate Council; and Francis X. Hogarty, Proctor.

Sixth row: Richard W. Warfield 1930, Assistant Personnel Director; Alexander Leitch 1924, Secretary to the President; William B. Van Alstyne, Jr., 1927, Personnel Director; and Datus C. Smith, Jr., 1929, Editor, *Princeton Alumni Weekly*.

President Dodds and Trustees, 1946. The trustees are standing on the steps of Chancellor Green Library which contains the Trustees Room.

Front row, left to right: Donald Danforth 1920; Stephen F. Voorhees 1900; Albert G. Milbank 1896; President Dodds; and Archibald A. Gulick 1897. Second row: Albridge C. Smith 1903; Dean Mathey 1912; Paul Bedford 1897; John Stuart 1900; and David A. Reed 1900. Third row: Robert Garrett 1897; Henry J. Cochran 1900; Chauncey Belknap 1912; Allen O. Whipple 1904; Alfred T. Carton 1905; and Fordyce B. St. John 1905.

Fourth row: David H. McAlpin 1920; Vice President Brakeley 1907; Franklin D'Olier 1898; Gordon S. Rentschler 1907; E. S. Wells Kerr 1909; and Frederick H. Osborn 1910. Back row: Richard F. Cleveland 1919; James C. Rea 1904; W. Logan MacCoy 1906; Ernest C. Savage 1919; and Henry P. Van Dusen 1919.

President and Vice President. The old office of Vice President that lapsed when John Maclean became President was revived in 1939 when GEORGE A. BRAKELEY 1907 was called to the re-created post. His title is now Vice President and Treasurer, and his role is largely that of fund raising, handling finances, and generally supervising the physical side of the University. Mr. Brakeley came to Princeton from the University of Pennsylvania where he held a similar post.

The picture was taken in President Dodds' office in Nassau Hall.

A Conference in Industrial Relations. The Industrial Relations Section, now in its third decade, has won an enviable reputation for its research publications and for the many services which it provides both for the University and for outside organizations. Here Director J. Douglas Brown 1919 (facing the camera) presides at a seminar in labor problems attended by a group of corporation executives engaged in personnel work.

PHOTO BY MENZIES

Staff Conference of the Princeton Surveys. The Princeton Surveys, founded in 1935, bring the best results of academic research into the functions of everyday government. The Surveys make their special studies in local government and taxation available to interested groups, and have exerted a considerable influence on state legislation.

Here a staff conference considers a thorny question of state taxation. From left to right: Miss Bernice Cloutier, librarian; Joseph E. McLean, research associate; Professor William S. Carpenter, chairman of the state Civil Service Commission; Professor John F. Sly, Director of the Surveys; Miss Barbara L. M. Sprott, executive secretary; Paul M. Douglas, research assistant; Miss Isobel Muirhead, research associate; and James A. Arnold, Jr., research associate.

Wartime Academic Procession, 1942. Honorary degrees had an Allied flavor in 1942. The academic procession, from right to left, is headed by President Dodds; Harlan F. Stone, Chief Justice of the United States; Wilson Farrand 1886, trustee; Dr. Hu Shih, the Chinese Ambassador; Dean Robert R. Wicks; and Lord Halifax, the British Ambassador.

PHOTO FROM PRESS ASSOCIATION, INC

President Dodds and Thomas Mann. Thomas Mann, distinguished author and winner of the Nobel Prize for literature, was a visiting lecturer at Princeton in 1938; he received the degree of Doctor of Letters.

President Dodds. A recent portrait.

CLEAROSE STUDIO

Buildings and Views

OLD CHEMICAL LABORATORY. This fortress-like structure was built in 1891, and for forty years undergraduates unflinchingly endured its pervasive smells. It is now used as an annex by the School of Engineering.

FIRST ISABELLA McCOSH INFIRMARY. Mrs. McCosh was closely interested in the health of the student body, and she personally nursed many an undergraduate. President McCosh repeatedly urged the trustees to provide an infirmary, and this building, opened in 1893, was named in her honor. Outgrown, despite extensions, it was replaced in 1925 by the new Isabella McCosh Infirmary.

ALBERT B. DOD HALL. This dormitory, erected in 1890, has fortunately had its rather harsh exterior softened by ivy. Named after Professor Albert B. Dod 1822, distinguished mathematician, it stands as an indication of the trustees' willingness to experiment with different architectural types.

DAVID BROWN HALL. Built in 1891 in the shape of a Florentine palace, this dormitory marked one of the last experiments with different styles of architecture before the trustees finally settled on English Gothic.

A. W. RICHARDS

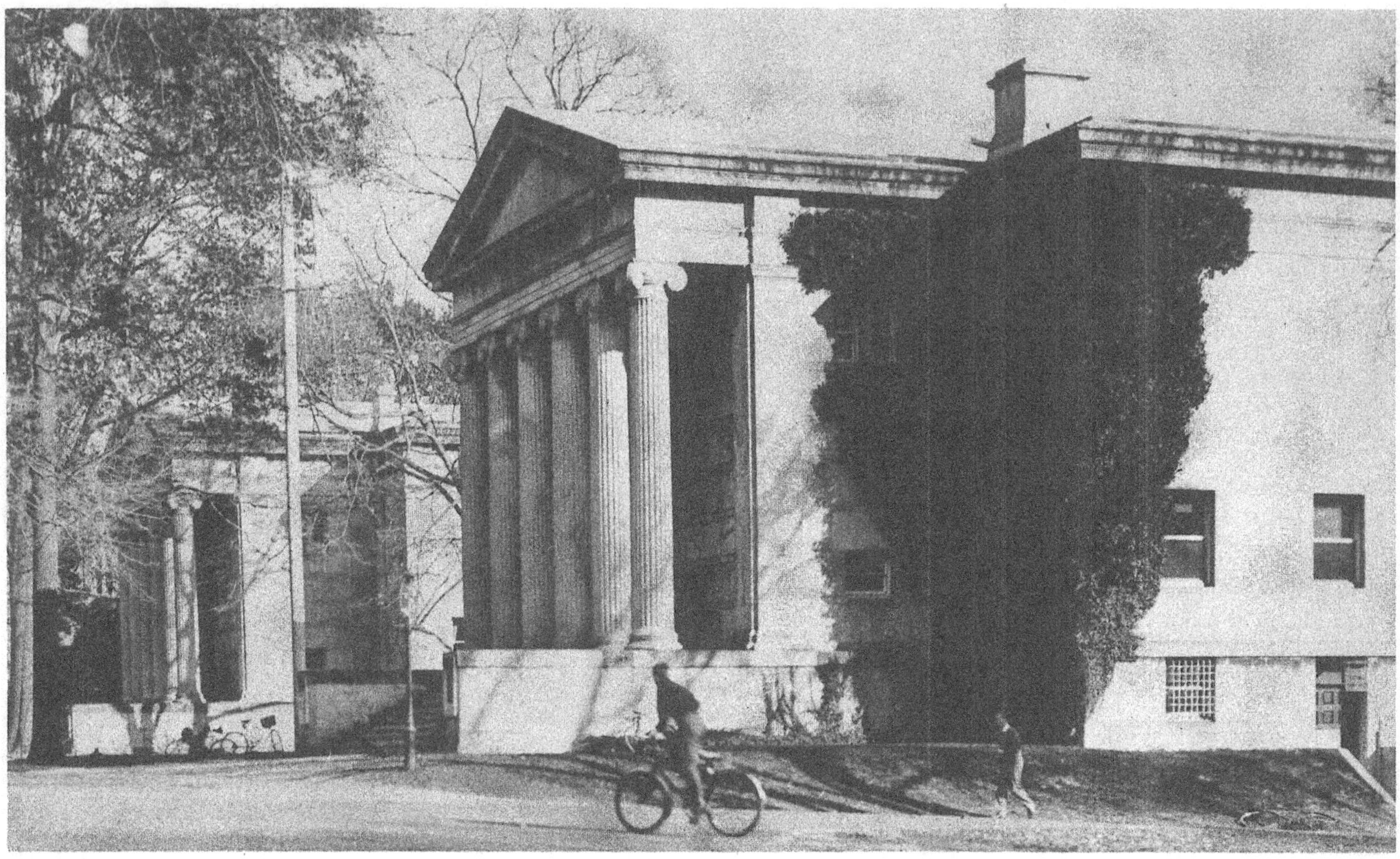

A. W. RICHARDS

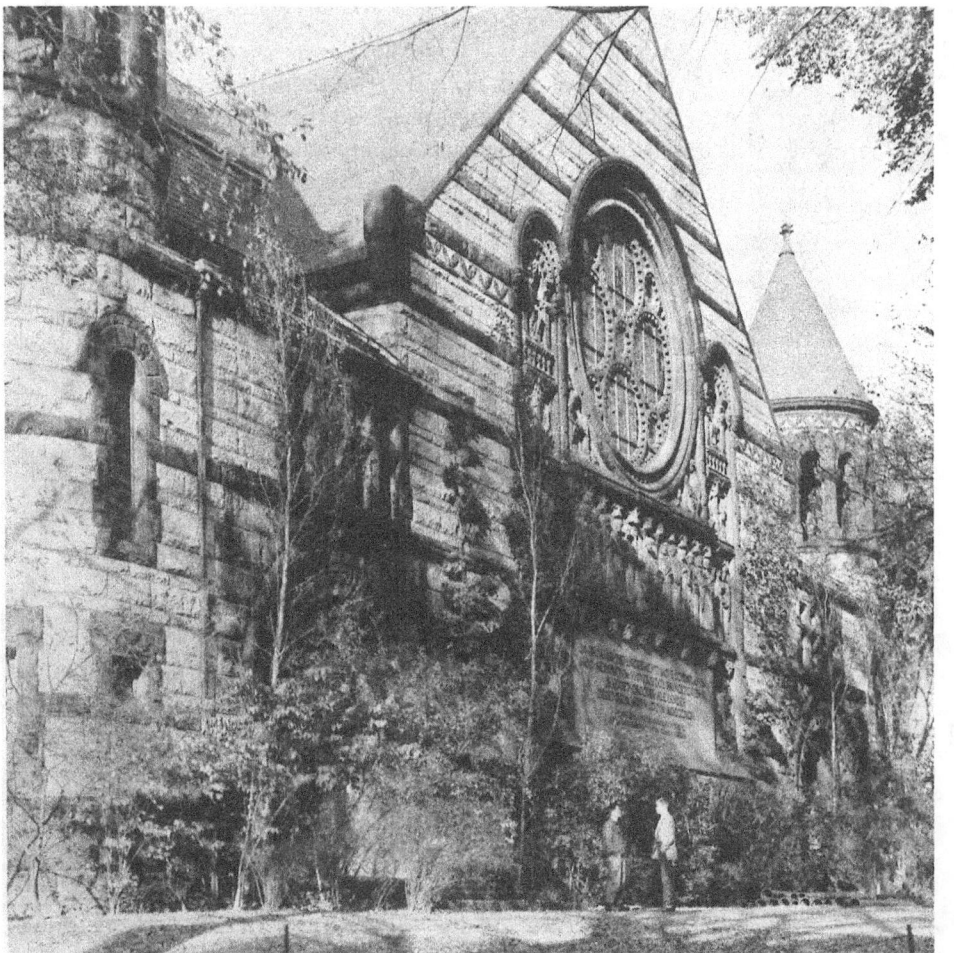

The Halls. In 1893 the old stucco structures of the Cliosophic and American Whig Societies were replaced with marble buildings. Although preserving the same appearance, they were moved closer together, so that the two walks from Nassau Street, instead of leading to their steps, now passed to the sides.

A. W. RICHARDS

Alexander Hall has served since 1894 as a general auditorium, and temporarily for a chapel (after Marquand burned). Its Romanesque design with Byzantine overtones, by William A. Potter, seems curious today but was greeted with satisfaction in the 1890's.

WEST SIDE OF CAMPUS, 1895. The clustered houses of Railroad Avenue (University Place) overlook the railroad station and the bare stretch of campus. At that time Alexander Hall was the most recent of the College buildings.

UPPER PYNE. This dormitory, with its counterpart, Lower Pyne, was the gift of Moses T. Pyne 1877. This view was made in 1897 soon after it was opened, long before the days of Palmer Square.

PYNE LIBRARY, and the **LIBRARY ARCHWAY.** The sesquicentennial gift of Mrs. Percy R. Pyne, the Library was built on ground formerly occupied by East College. Fifty years later the increase of volumes, together with the outmoded design, made it obsolete.

PHOTO BY LEIGH

BLAIR HALL. The gift of John I. Blair, railroad capitalist, Blair Hall was the first dormitory to be built in Tudor Gothic. Designed by Cope and Stewardson, Blair set the style followed by all dormitories since 1897. This view, from the southwest, shows Blair Arch which formerly served as the west entrance to the campus. The old railroad station, until 1918, stood in the foreground; and an old milestone, marked "Zero," stands as its only reminder.

STAFFORD LITTLE HALL. Built south of Blair in two sections, in 1899 and 1901, Little, with Blair, marked the then western limit of the campus. This is the northern section, from the west. It was the first dormitory to have bathrooms.

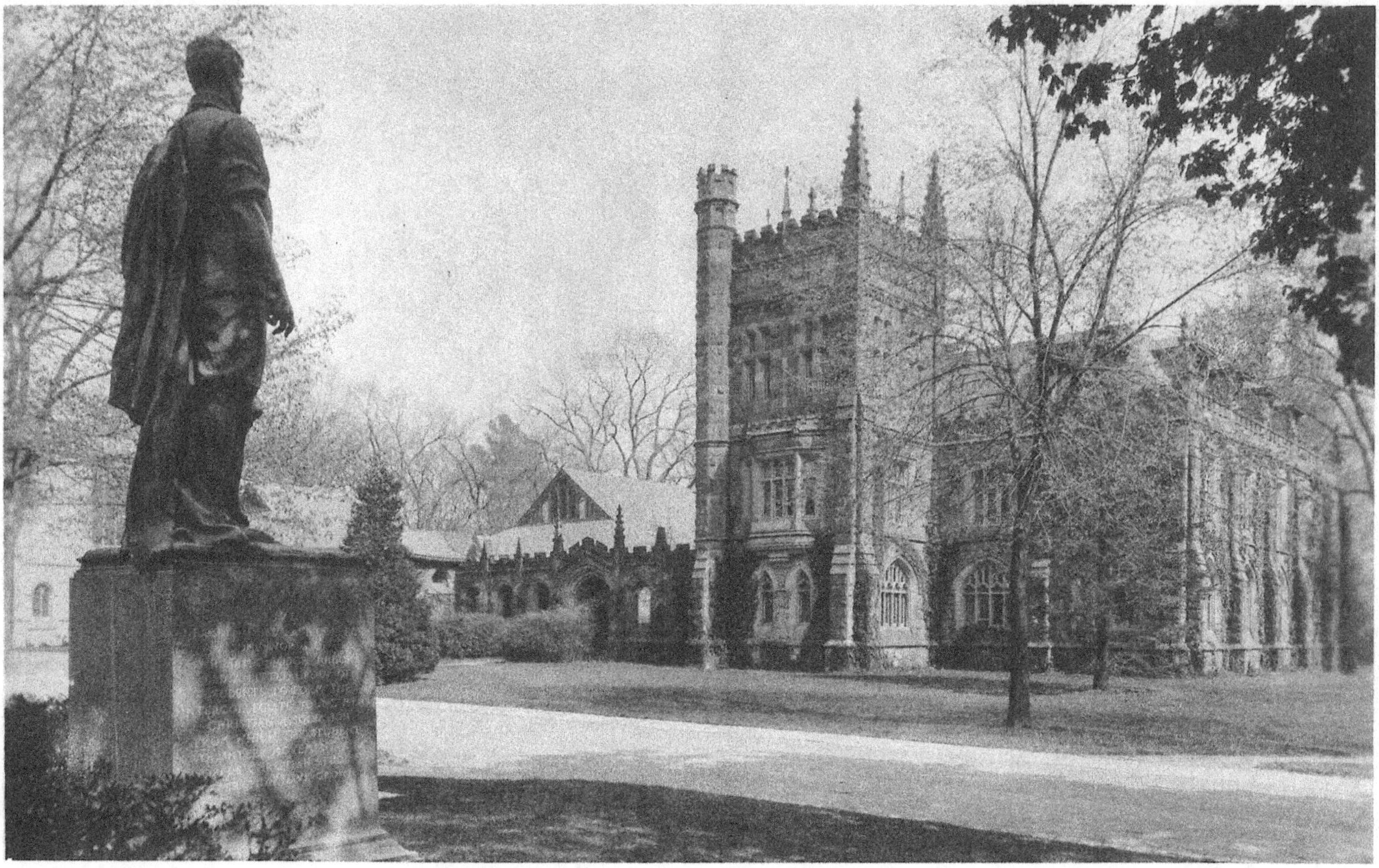

ORREN JACK TURNER

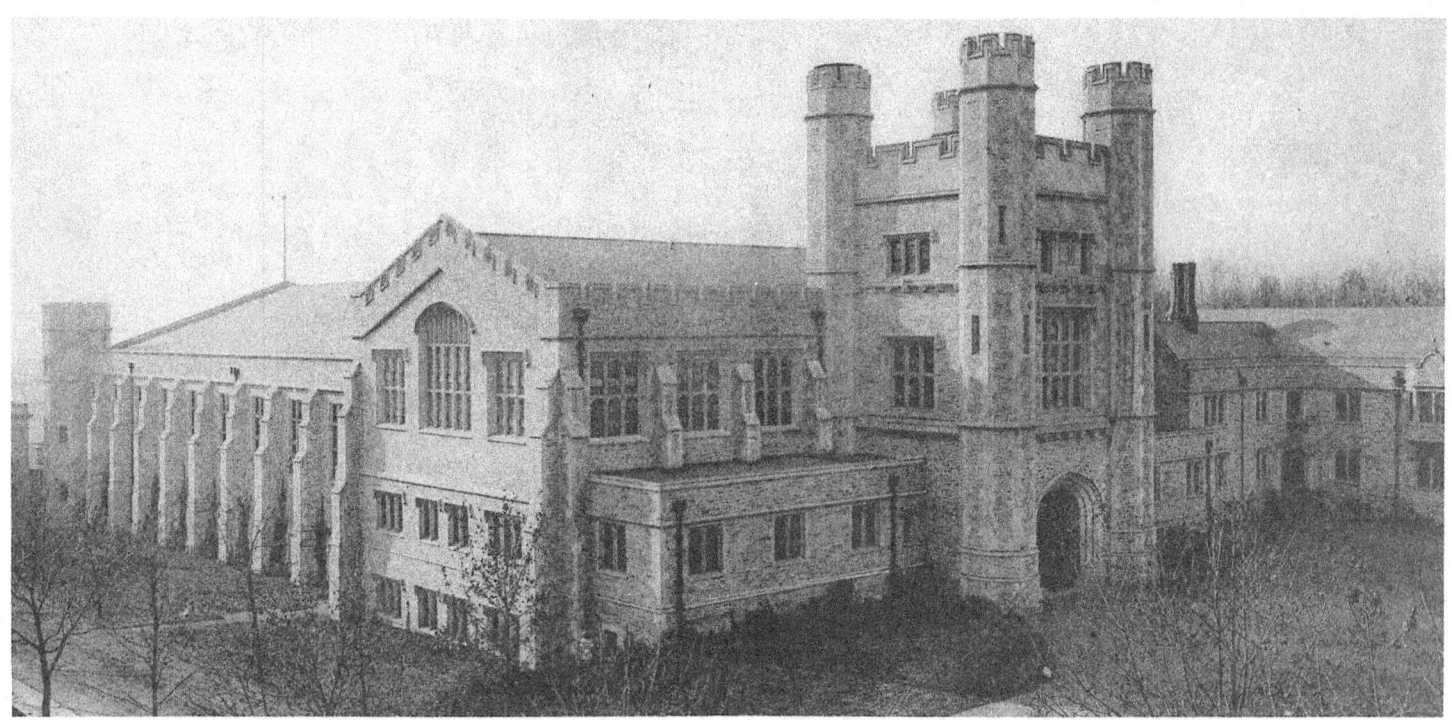

MURRAY DODGE HALL. These two connected buildings comprise the Murray Theatre (on the left) 1879 and Dodge Hall 1900. The former is the headquarters of the Theatre Intime, the latter long housed the Philadelphian Society and since World War II serves as the campus social center.

The Christian Student, facing south from Pyne Library, was the work of Daniel Chester French. It disappeared from the campus some years ago, after an undergraduate riot.

OLD GYMNASIUM. Built in 1903, it replaced the Bonner Gymnasium. For four decades it gáve yeoman service, and two generations of Princetonians remember it with affection. It burned in 1944, to be replaced by the Dillon Gymnasium.

THE FACULTY ROOM of Nassau Hall is one of the most beautiful and dignified rooms in America. Originally the old prayer hall, it was remodeled as the Faculty Room in 1906. The seats follow the English parliamentary arrangement.

SEVENTY-NINE HALL. The only dormitory on the east side of the campus, it was presented to the University by the Class of 1879 in 1904. Over the archway are offices built especially for Woodrow Wilson 1879, when he was President.

PATTON HALL. Erected in honor of former President Francis Landey Patton in 1906, this is the southernmost dormitory of the University. The rooms in its high tower are eagerly sought by undergraduates.

PALMER PHYSICAL LABORATORY. Some of the outstanding physical research in both World Wars was carried out within its walls. This view, from the south, was taken from Guyot Hall. It was the gift of Stephen S. Palmer, in 1908.

CORNER OF McCOSH HALL. This building, erected in 1907, is the University's principal hall for lecture rooms and preceptorial conferences. During the class periods it disgorges and swallows over a thousand students every hour. The Mather Sun Dial is near the center of the great quadrangle formed by McCosh, Dickinson, and the Chapel.

GUYOT HALL. Constructed in 1909, Guyot Hall houses extensive laboratories and museums of the Biology and Geology Departments. Named for Princeton's famous geographer, Arnold H. Guyot, it was given by the Dodge family.

CAMPBELL HALL. Erected south of Holder Hall in 1909, this dormitory faces Blair on the south. Joline Hall, built in 1932, connects it with the "Little Arch" of Blair. The spires of Holder Tower are seen over the roofline.

Turning the Sod for Holder Tower. Holder Hall was the gift of Mrs. Russell Sage, and is shown here partially completed. In 1910 presentation ceremonies were held, and ground was turned for Holder Tower, also given by Mrs. Sage. In this picture President Wilson, with the spade, listens as Robert W. de Forest makes the formal presentation.

Holder Hall and Tower. The northwest corner of Holder court, with the Cloisters on the left. This section of the campus was originally the burial ground of the FitzRandolph family, in the eighteenth century. It was Nathaniel FitzRandolph who gave the land on which Nassau Hall was erected. Holder Hall was named in honor of Christopher Holder, a Quaker ancestor of Mrs. Sage.

E. W. ROTHE

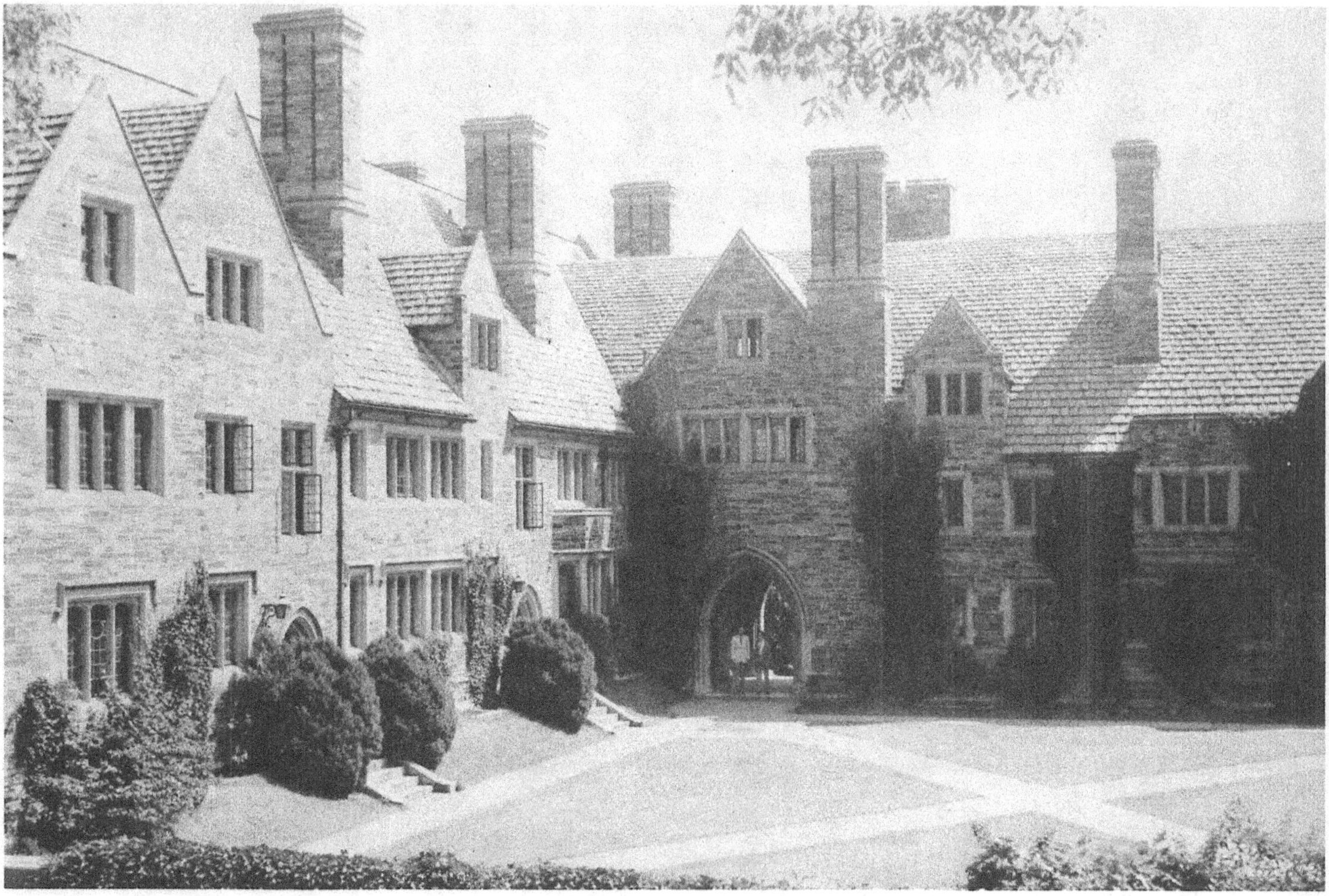

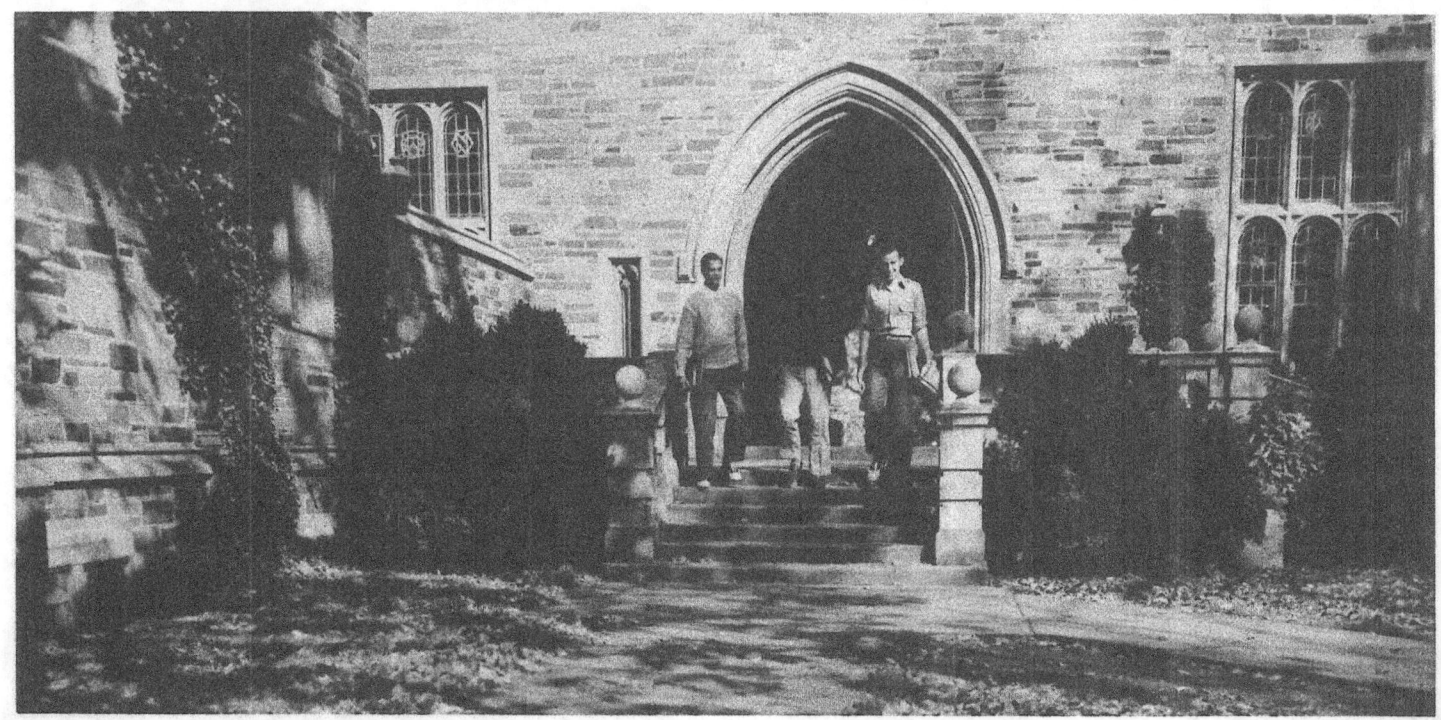

CUYLER HALL. This dormitory was designed by Day and Klauder, who did some of the finest work in modified Gothic to be found on the campus. Erected in 1912 on a site north of Patton, it was named for Cornelius C. Cuyler 1879.

A. W. RICHARDS

HAMILTON COURT. Hamilton Hall, adjoining Holder on the west side, was built in 1911 in honor of Governor John Hamilton who granted Princeton's first charter in 1746. It has a small but lovely court.

A. W. RICHARDS

GRADUATE COLLEGE, from the West. The Graduate College was dedicated in 1913, and was the fruit of long effort by Dean West and others to create an institution with outstanding facilities for graduate work. It was designed by Cram, Goodhue, and Ferguson.

The main quadrangle is Thomson College. Cleveland Tower is near the entrance, while extending from the lower right corner of the quadrangle is Procter Hall with the great Memorial Window. In the right foreground is Wyman House, residence of the Dean of the Graduate School.

Across the golf links is the Princeton Inn.

GRADUATE COLLEGE ENTRANCE. Bicycling is the favorite means of transportation between the Graduate College and the campus, a mile away.

87

A. W. RICHARDS

AERIAL VIEW OF THE GRADUATE COLLEGE, from the southwest of Cleveland Tower, looking toward the Golf Club, the buildings of the Theological Seminary and the University campus. The Tower, 173 feet high, was named for Grover Cleveland, long chairman of the Trustees' Committee on the Graduate School; it was erected by public subscription as a memorial. The Class of 1892 Memorial Carillon is hung in the Tower.

The small quadrangle, to the north of Thomson College, was built in 1926. This quadrangle and Procter Hall were the gifts of William C. Procter 1883.

MADISON HALL. The five University dining halls are known collectively as Madison Hall, which was built in 1916 on the site of the old University Hall. This view, from University Place, caught Albert M. Friend 1915, Professor of Art and Archaeology, in a guarded moment. Madison Hall was designed by Day and Klauder.

PYNE HALL. Pyne was the first of the new dormitories built in the southwest section of the campus, in 1922. The private houses lining the east side of University Place were gradually acquired and removed, permitting a large development in that area. Pyne Hall was named in honor of Moses T. Pyne 1877, Princeton's great benefactor.

SOUTHWESTERN ENTRANCE TO THE CAMPUS. Arriving by train, the visitor usually enters the campus through this gateway between 1901 Hall (right) and 1904-Henry Hall (left). Princeton has long been known for its beautiful landscape gardening, and the yews lining this entrance greatly add to its attractiveness. PYNE HALL is in the right foreground.

1905-FOULKE HALL. This dormitory was erected in 1923 on University Place, just north of 1904-Henry. It was named in memory of three members of the Class of 1905 who died i World War I. The main walk leads to Blair Steps.

McCARTER THEATER. The gift of the Triangle Club and Thomas N. McCarter 1888, McCarter Theater was erected in 1929. Triangle and Broadway productions are shown here, and the University uses it for special convocations. This picture was taken at a Reunion, when the Class of 1922 had posted its numerals on the east side.

CLASS OF 1901 AND LAUGHLIN HALLS. These adjoining dormitories, built in 1926, parallel the main walk that leads through the new dormitories to Blair. Day and Klauder were the architects of these two halls.

LOCKHART HALL. Lockhart Hall was built in 1927 on University Place. This rear view was taken from Blair Arch. Lockhart was the last of the six dormitories to be built in the southwestern area of the campus.

WALKER HALL. After the southwestern section had been covered with dormitories, the University turned to the south central area. Walker Hall was built in 1929, just north of the tennis courts. With Patton, it marks the southern boundary of campus dormitories. It was the gift of the family of James T. Walker 1927.

ORREN JACK TURNER

CLASS OF 1903 HALL. This dormitory, the gift of the Class of 1903, was built in 1929 just east of Cuyler Hall, which completes the quadrangle. Its court is one of the beauty spots of the campus.

McCORMICK HALL. This example of Siennese Gothic faces west from the Museum of Historic Art with which it is connected. The two house the Department of Art and Archaeology and the School of Architecture. In addition to class halls and drafting rooms, McCormick contains the Marquand Library of art. It was the gift of the McCormick family in 1921.

ENO HALL, built in 1924 as the workshop for Princeton's psychologists, has the distinction of being the only college psychological laboratory in America constructed as a separate building with its own planned facilities. The Department of Psychology has grown so much, however, that plans call for its future enlargement.

ISABELLA McCOSH INFIRMARY. This Infirmary, opened in 1925, was built on the site of its predecessor. The several sun parlors are sometimes used as galleries by the inmates when an exciting tennis match is in progress.

THE UNIVERSITY CHAPEL. Completed in 1928, the Chapel is one of the most beautiful Gothic buildings in America. It stands as a monument to the administration of President Hibben, who worked untiringly for its erection and for whom the Hibben Nave is named. The Chapel was designed by Cram and Ferguson, and was built by many individual gifts.

THE INTERIOR OF THE CHAPEL, opposite. The Hibben Nave and Milbank Choir, looking toward the east window. The stained glass of the chapel is considered by critics the finest ensemble of this art to be found in America. The space and dignity of the interior impress the most casual visitor. The Chapel is 249 feet long, while the width of the nave is over 61 feet. It seats 1800 persons. Despite its large size, it is not out of proportion to the surrounding buildings.

JOHN C. GREEN ENGINEERING BUILDING was erected in 1928 on the east side of Washington Road, replacing the old School of Science as the headquarters of the School of Engineering. Its south side flanks William Street, and a general expansion of the building to the rear is planned to increase its facilities.

HENRY CLAY FRICK CHEMICAL LABORATORY was opened in 1929, supplanting the old Laboratory originally built in 1891. The general design was similar to that of the Engineering Building, both having the same architect, Charles Z. Klauder. Construction of these two opened a new area for expansion of the campus on the east side of Washington Road.

THE NEW OBSERVATORY, erected east of the Stadium in 1934, replaced the old Halsted Observatory that had long stood on the west side of the campus, near the Little Arch of Blair. The material of the old building was used for the new one.

FINE HALL, built in 1931 in honor of the late Dean Henry B. Fine, is the center for Princeton's famous Department of Mathematics. It has also been extensively used by members of the Institute for Advanced Study. It is connected with Palmer Physical Laboratory. This view shows Proctor Michael C. Kopliner coming around the corner.

PRINCETON UNIVERSITY PRESS. The Gothic building in which the University Press is housed was the gift of Charles Scribner 1875. Erected in 1911, the same year that the Press was organized in its present form as a non-profit organization, it contains editorial offices and its own printing plant. Some seven hundred books have been published to date, as well as the *Annals of Mathematics*, *The Public Opinion Quarterly* and the *Princeton Alumni Weekly*.

THE NASSAU CLUB. Founded in 1889 as a faculty and alumni social organization, the Nassau Club has become one of Princeton's most famous institutions. Its early quarters were in the old University Hall; but in 1903, when Woodrow Wilson was president of the Club, the house built in 1813 by the Reverend Samuel Miller was purchased. Its dining rooms have witnessed innumerable faculty conferences; and it has also served as the last retreat of bachelors.

A. W. RICHARDS

AIR VIEWS OF THE CAMPUS, taken from a plane in the summer of 1946.

The northwestern section of the campus, shown above, invariably reminds the visitor of Oxford. On the north side of Nassau Street are the buildings of Palmer Square.

The southwestern quarter, at the left, includes McCarter Theater. The high walls are acquiring a patina of ivy.

An eastward sweep of the north campus, on the right, with the chapel in the background. Nassau Street is almost hidden by elms and sycamores.

The campus from the south, below right, is bordered by various playing fields. Baker Rink is in the foreground.

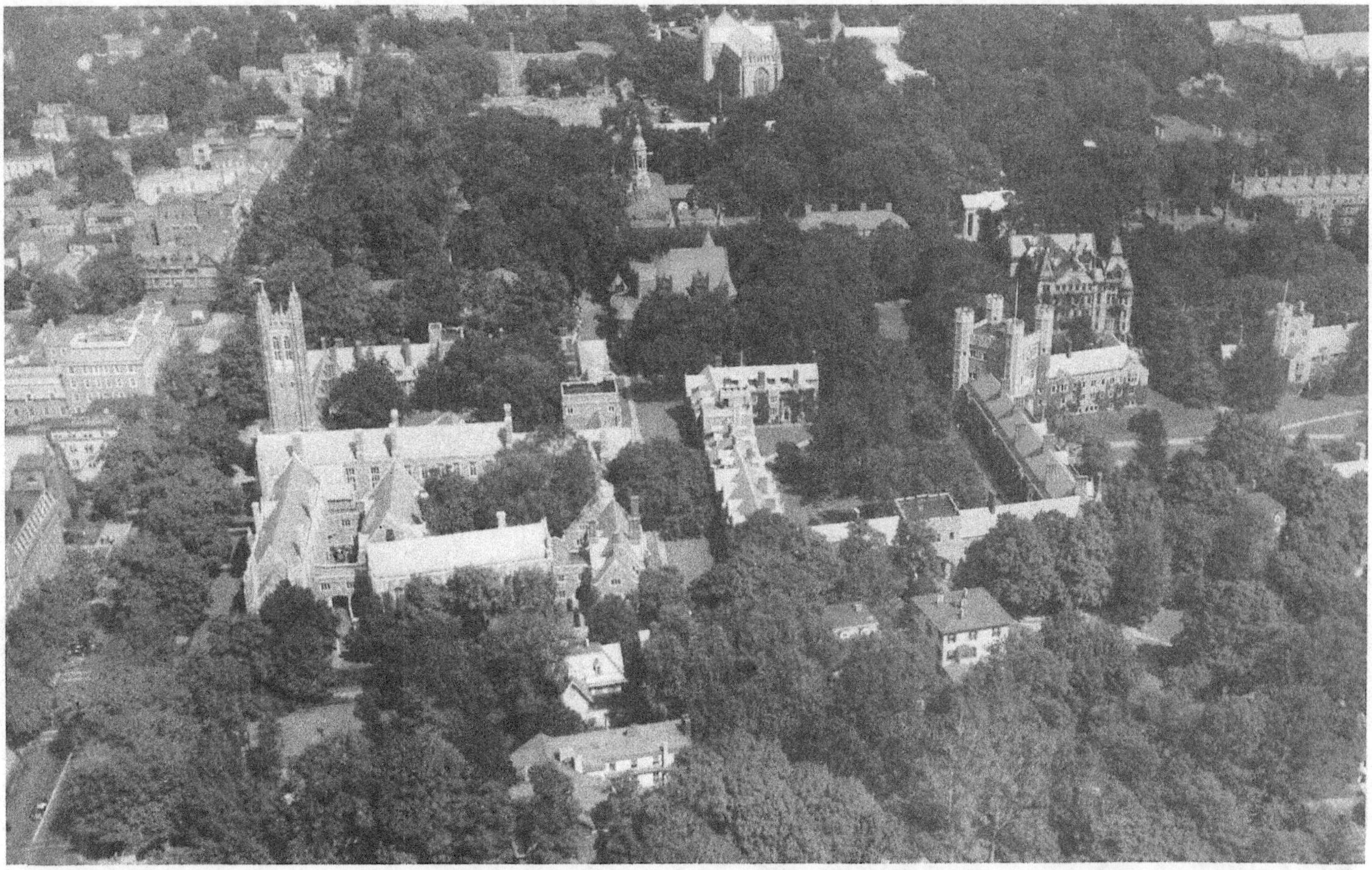

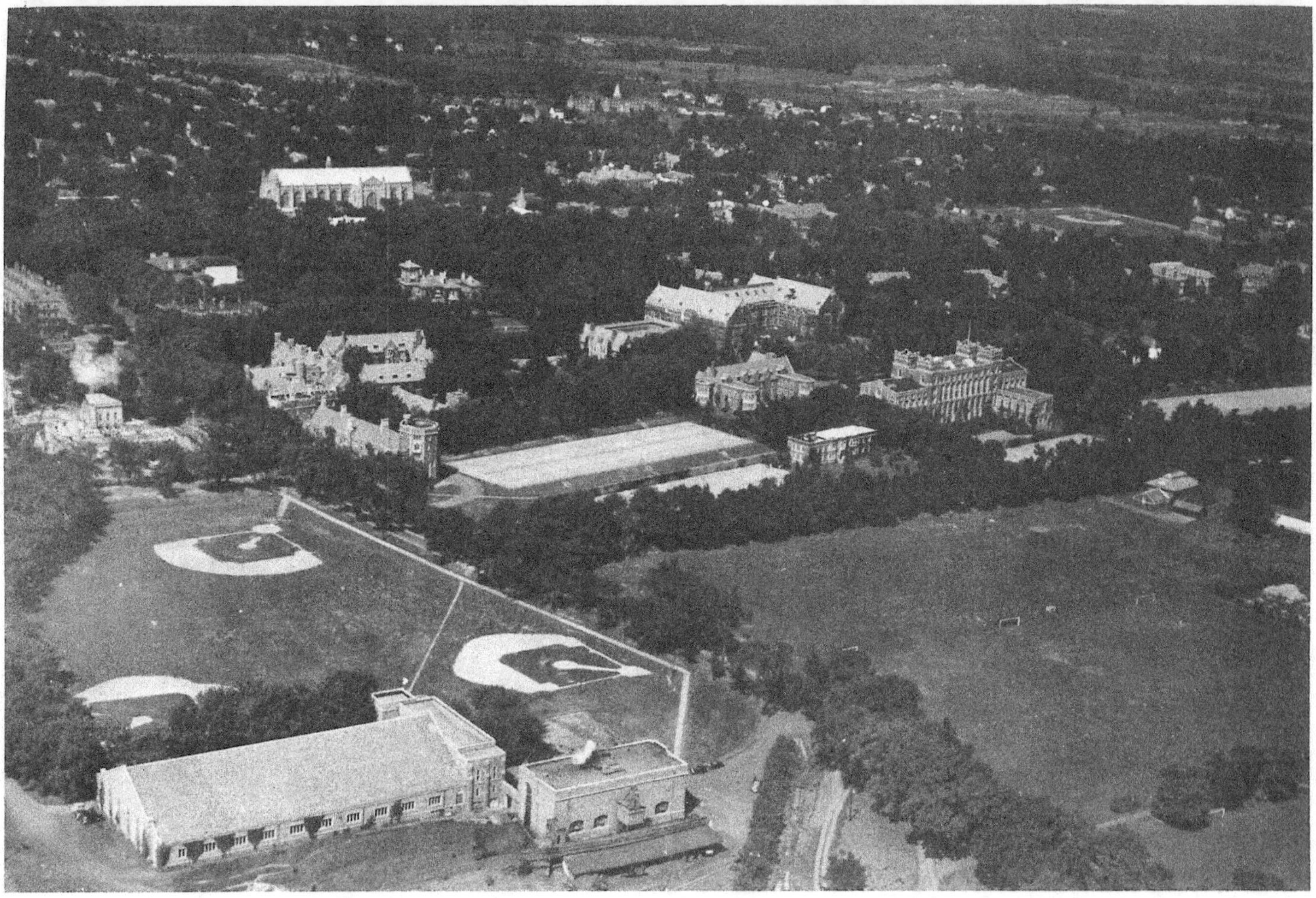

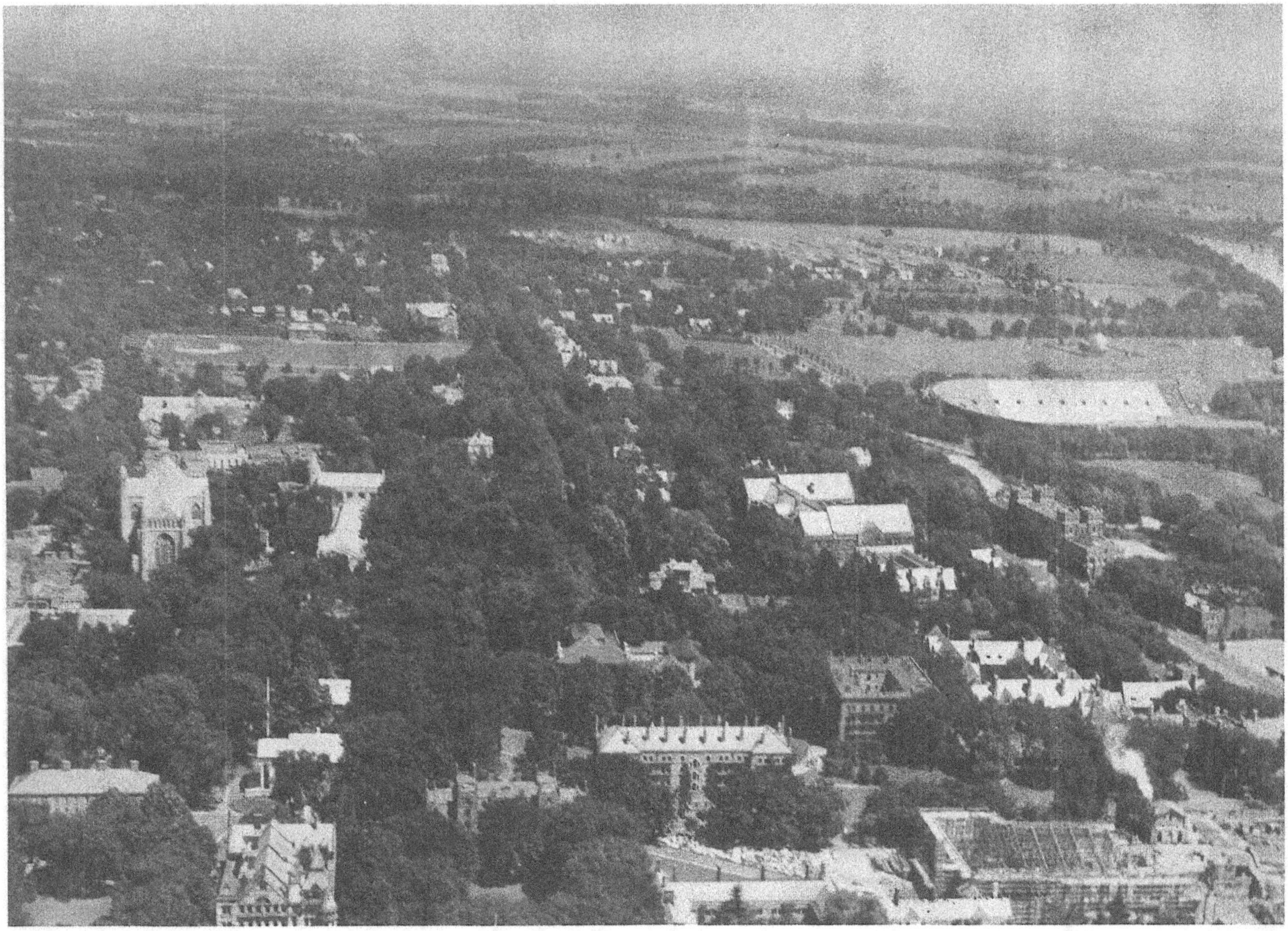

A. W. RICHARDS

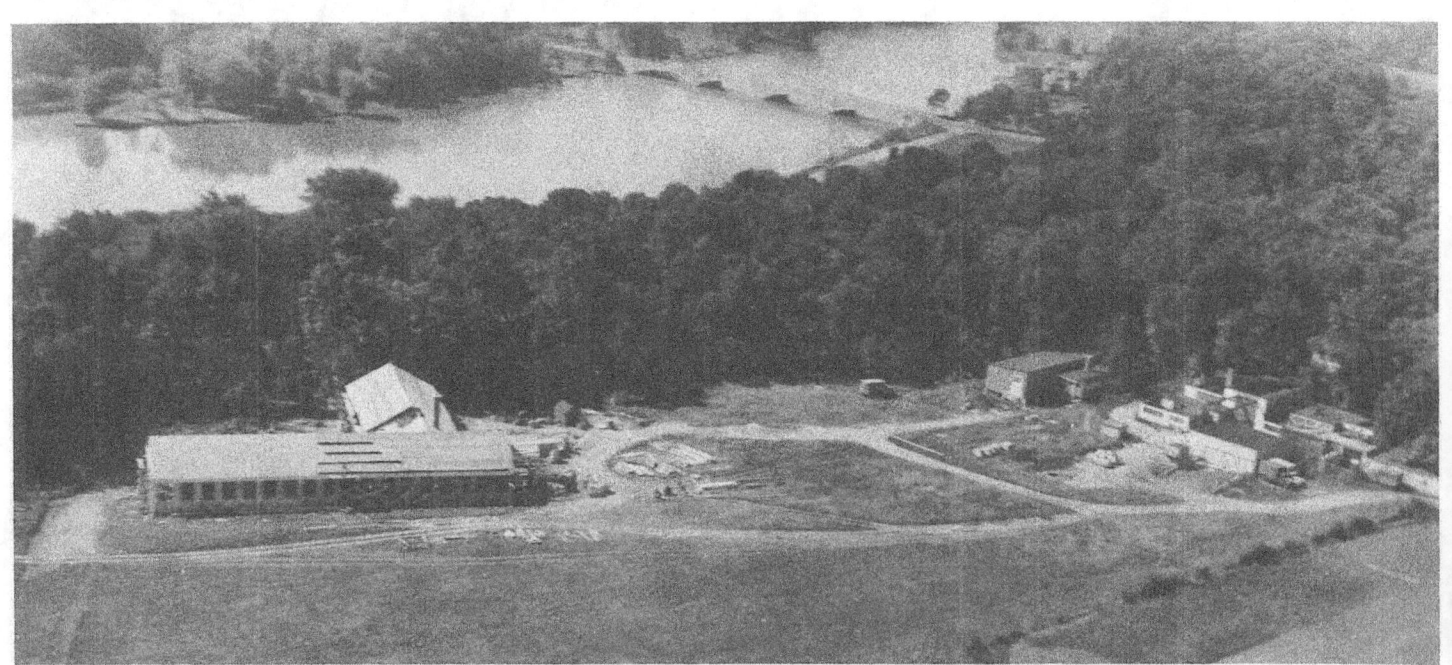

SOUTHEASTERN SECTION OF THE CAMPUS. The gently sloping coastal plain of New Jersey is readily apparent in this view. In the right foreground is the new Herbert L. Dillon Gymnasium under construction.

A. W. RICHARDS

BORDER OF THE LAKE. The area southeast of the Stadium is the scene of various scientific and engineering developments. Here the Naval Research Laboratory is under construction (left), and "Project Squid" progresses (right).

EAST ELEVATION OF THE DILLON GYMNASIUM. The gift of Herbert L. Dillon 1907, it was designed by Aymar Embury 1900.

NEW SWIMMING POOL. Located on the south side of the Gymnasium, the pool has a color scheme of orange and black.

HERBERT LOWELL DILLON GYMNASIUM. Princeton's new Gymnasium approaching completion, in the spring of 1947.

EXCAVATION FOR THE HARVEY S. FIRESTONE MEMORIAL LIBRARY. Tons of rock had to blasted out for the three stories below ground level. This view, in early 1946, is the last to show the Class of 1877 Laboratory, (soon demolished).

ARCHITECT'S DRAWING OF THE FIRESTONE LIBRARY. Designed by Robert B. O'Connor and Walter H. Kilham, Jr., the new Library, to be completed in 1948, will incorporate many features to make it functionally adapted to a modern university. A modular plan of design makes the building adaptable to changing needs and conditions. Its stacks will be open.

Princeton in War

The major wars of American history have affected Princeton profoundly. In the Revolution the College necessarily had to cease operations during the early part of 1777, and during the Civil War the undergraduate body was greatly depleted. In the two World Wars the University was almost completely militarized and converted into a training camp for the armed forces. The record of Princeton men in the service of their country is a proud one; altogether some 17,000 Princeton alumni and students have served in one or more wars.

The Revolution, of course, came closest to Princeton, both literally and figuratively. Apart from the fact that the campus became a battlefield, the College was intimately connected with the Revolutionary movement. Under Witherspoon the students expressed their determination to support the cause of American liberties. They boycotted British goods, and had their own tea party. Witherspoon himself and many of the trustees became outstanding figures in the Whig cause. With the approach of hostilities, the students organized a company of fifty men which later marched away to war. Ten Princetonians died in the struggle.

The last phase of the Battle of Princeton took place on the campus. The British, defeated near Stony Brook, retreated to Princeton village and some of them attempted to hold out in Nassau Hall. Cannonfire from the artillery of Alexander Hamilton soon led them to surrender, however, and they laid down their weapons on the front campus, a "haughty, crabbed set of men." For years Nassau Hall, with gaping holes in her walls, showed the effects of the Battle.

The approach of the Civil War was particularly distressing to Princeton because one-third of the students came from the slave-holding states. Many northern undergraduates supported the southerners in their demonstrations against abolitionist agitation, and when war came there were many sad farewells at the railroad station as the southern boys departed, some to face their classmates on the field of battle. About 433 alumni served in the war; and thirty-five gave their lives fighting for the Union, and the same number for the Confederacy.

In World War I Princeton was transformed into a training school in which civilians almost entirely disappeared. Even before the country entered the war, the students had asked for and entered upon military training of an elective nature. A Provisional Battalion was organized in February 1917. With the declaration of war, large numbers of undergraduates enlisted or else remained to enter the School of Military Aeronautics, the Naval Training Unit, or the Students' Army Training Corps. Over half the faculty was on leave for military service or special war research. Altogether 6,170 Princeton men were in military service in the war, of whom 151 were killed.

In World War II Princeton once more gave its entire self to the war effort. Including the special schools which both Army and Navy organized and operated with their own personnel, a total of some 20,000 men received military training at Princeton. Including former graduate students, 10,054 Princeton men were in the service, of whom 354 gave their lives. And as before, the faculty achieved a notable record of accomplishment, many of them leaving for the service and others remaining to carry the heavy load of extra teaching or to engage in scientific research of a military nature.

WASHINGTON AT THE BATTLE OF PRINCETON. This famous painting, one of the University's prize possessions, has hung in Nassau Hall since 1784. It depicts Washington at the close of the Battle. Nassau Hall is revealed in the background, as seen from the south, while in the foreground General Hugh Mercer lies mortally wounded.

Washington was a benefactor of Princeton, bestowing fifty guineas on the institution when he was there in the summer of 1783. Not to be outdone, the trustees asked Washington to sit for his portrait to be painted by Charles Willson Peale, so that it might hang in Nassau Hall in place of the picture of "his late majesty." The portrait of George II had been destroyed by a cannon-shot in the Battle. Washington agreed, and the canvas was placed in the frame that formerly held the portrait of the king. The portrait was formally hung at the commencement in 1784 when Peale was a guest of honor.

THE HISTORICAL SOCIETY OF PENNSYLVANIA

THE BATTLE OF PRINCETON, January 3, 1777. The Battle has long been studied by military strategists as the classic example of how a general whose forces were hopelessly outnumbered surprised the enemy by marching around to his rear, thus forcing him to retreat. The picture shows Washington's troops advancing and firing on the enemy in the region just east of Stony Brook. In the foreground is Washington with a few of his staff, while in the center is a prostrate white horse whose rider has been wounded. This officer is undoubtedly General Hugh Mercer, who was wounded in the Battle and who died in the Clarke House depicted in the background. From this battlefield the American troops advanced to the center of Princeton where the British sought refuge behind the thick walls of Nassau Hall.

This picture was painted soon after the Revolution by William Mercer, son of the officer killed in the Battle.

REOPENING OF COLLEGE. John Witherspoon requests the undergraduates "to repair to Princeton without delay," now that the British have left Princeton. It was probably wishful thinking that led him to hope that the students "had been pursuing their studies separately." (From *The Pennsylvania Evening Post* of June 26, 1777.)

Procession of students at Princeton College, escorting to the depot three of their number suspended for pumping a secessionist.

THE MARTYRS OF THE PUMP, 1861. By the fall of 1861 practically all southern sympathizers had withdrawn from Princeton. Francis DuBois, Jr., 1863, had the temerity to express his sympathy for the southern cause, however, and was placed under the college pump where "that venerable institution was put into operation and continued to pour forth its acqueous contents until the fire of disunion was pretty well quenched in his breast."

President Maclean and his faculty were unionist, but they felt they should not permit the students to take the law into their own hands; so three of the offending undergraduates were suspended. They were Howard J. Reeder 1863, Samuel B. Huey 1863, and Isaac K. Casey 1864. They are here shown being drawn triumphantly to the railroad station, in a flag-draped barouche, by their fellow students. All three later served with the Union forces.

CIVIL WAR CELEBRATION. The fall of Richmond was celebrated with a huge bonfire around the Cannon, fireworks, and the illumination of every house in town. Wrote the *Princeton Standard*, "Flags flying, handkerchiefs waving, windows blazing, torchlights burning, fireworks flying through the air, everyone shouting, horns sounding—who ever beheld such a time in the usually quiet, serene Princeton?"

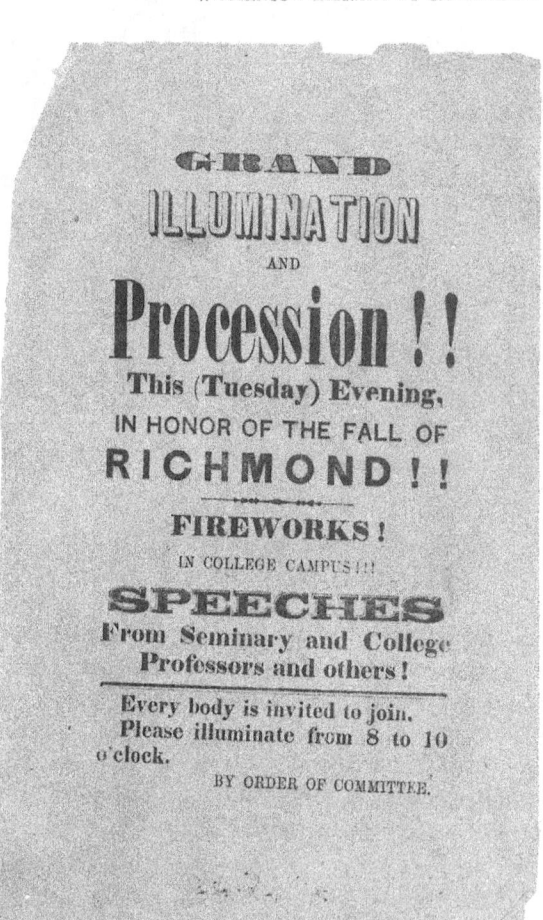

GRAND ILLUMINATION AND Procession!!
This (Tuesday) Evening,
IN HONOR OF THE FALL OF
RICHMOND!!
FIREWORKS!
IN COLLEGE CAMPUS!!!
SPEECHES
From Seminary and College Professors and others!
Every body is invited to join. Please illuminate from 8 to 10 o'clock.
BY ORDER OF COMMITTEE.

SPANISH-AMERICAN WAR, 1898. In 1898, when hostilities with Spain seemed imminent, a battalion of some four hundred undergraduates was organized. Drill was conducted with Professor William Libbey 1877 as drillmaster. The undergraduates are here shown marching vigorously on Brokaw Field in order to be ready when the call came. Professor Libbey also organized Company L, 2nd Regiment, of the New Jersey National Guard the same year. In this war, five Princeton men gave their lives.

PRINCETON FLYING SCHOOL. Princeton was designated as a Government Ground School in June 1917, but before that time undergraduates and interested alumni had set up a Flying School on an informal basis. Three planes were secured and a field out on Mercer Street was used by the fledgling aviators. This is an early 1917 view of the Flying School students, with one of their planes.

Front row, left to right: R. H. McCann 1917; F. J. Newbury, Jr., 1917; Wistar Morris 1919; H. M. Smith 1919; P. T. Morgan, Jr., 1920; C. R. Erdman, Jr., 1919; M. S. Quay 1919; W. B. Kelly 1919; J. F. Bohmfalk 1917; and E. M. Cronin 1917.

Kneeling: L. G. Kaye 1921; F. C. Burger 1919; Instructor Kenyon; L. C. Holden, Jr., 1919; F. A. Zunino, Jr., 1918; M. H. Pyne 1921; and C. H. Grant 1917.

Standing: W. H. Neely 1917; two mechanics; F. W. Sidley 1919; L. M. Sears 1918; unidentified; G. A. Vaughan, Jr., 1919; H. K. Bulkley 1919; Instructor E. R. Kennison; M. F. Mill 1902, who organized the Flying School; S. E. Brewster 1918; A. W. Bevin 1916; J. P. Hill 1919; B. H. Bostwick 1919; W. M. Broadway 1917; and Francis Callery 1920.

COMPANY L LEAVING PRINCETON, 1917. This Company, first organized at the time of the Spanish-American War, comprised both University and town personnel, there being thirty-five faculty members, alumni, or undergraduates in it. On March 30, 1917, Company L was called out to join its Regiment; here it marches by the Second Presbyterian Church.

ROSE AND SON

TRENCH WARFARE was an all-important subject in the SATC program. Sections of the south campus were quickly converted into elaborate systems of trenches by the 1001 members of the Students' Army Training Corps.

SATC DRILLING on Brokaw Field. The University was completely militarized by 1918. The Students' Army Training Corps and the Naval Training Unit took over, and the civilian undergraduate disappeared.

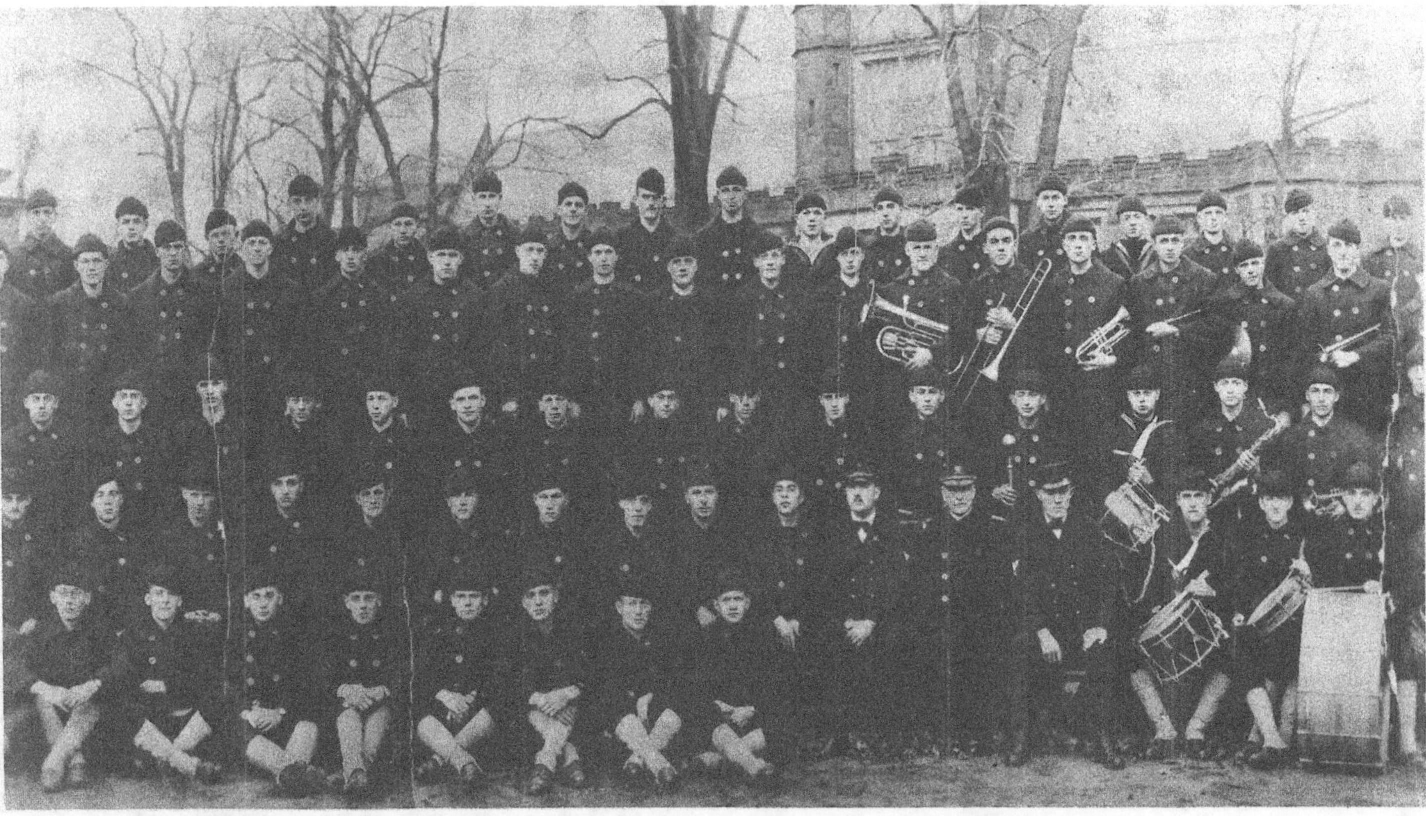

NAVAL TRAINING UNIT, 1918. This is a small section of the 330 men of the Naval Training Unit, the entire picture being too large to be reproduced here. The photograph was taken as the Unit was grouped around the Cannon. The Naval Training Unit, with the Officer Material School of the Navy Pay Corps, was commanded by Rear Admiral Caspar F. Goodrich, U.S.N. His staff for the Naval Training Unit consisted of only two chief petty officers, who here flank the Admiral.

PHOTO BY MENZIES

ACTION BY THE FIELD ARTILLERY, ROTC. Following World War I, a Reserve Officers Training Corps of the Field Artillery was established at Princeton. Graduates of the course were commissioned as second lieutenants and practically all saw service in World War II. The countryside, in the 1920's and 1930's, frequently reverberated with cannonfire when the artillerymen engaged in practice, which was held in the open fields near Lake Carnegie.

FIELD ARTILLERY PRACTICE. How about a little more camouflage for deception?

COMMUNICATIONS OPEN. Field Artillerymen communicating with a firing battery from an observation post.

SERVICE FLAG IN WORLD WAR II. A passing GI stops to look at the service flag which was flown during the war in front of Nassau Hall. The final figure for Princeton men in the service was 10,054, or over one-third of the living alumni and undergraduates; while 354 gave their lives fighting for their country in World War II.

A NEW GROUP OF LIEUTENANTS. President Dodds speaking to newly commissioned officers at commencement, 1942.

R. V. C. WHITEHEAD, JR.

PHOTO BY MENZIES

WARTIME LEADERS AT PRINCETON. Seated in front of Reunion Hall are Col. Arthur E. Fox 1913, head of the Army training program; President Dodds; and Capt. Geoffrey Sage, in charge of Navy units. Other commanding officers appeared from time to time, but these two officers remained the longest at the helm.

A WELCOME GIFT. The Aeronautical Engineering Department expanded greatly during the war. In 1944 its equipment was augmented by an autogiro, the gift of Harvey S. Firestone, Jr., 1920. Left to right are Professor Daniel C. Sayre, Mr. Firestone, President Dodds, and Dean Kenneth H. Condit 1913.

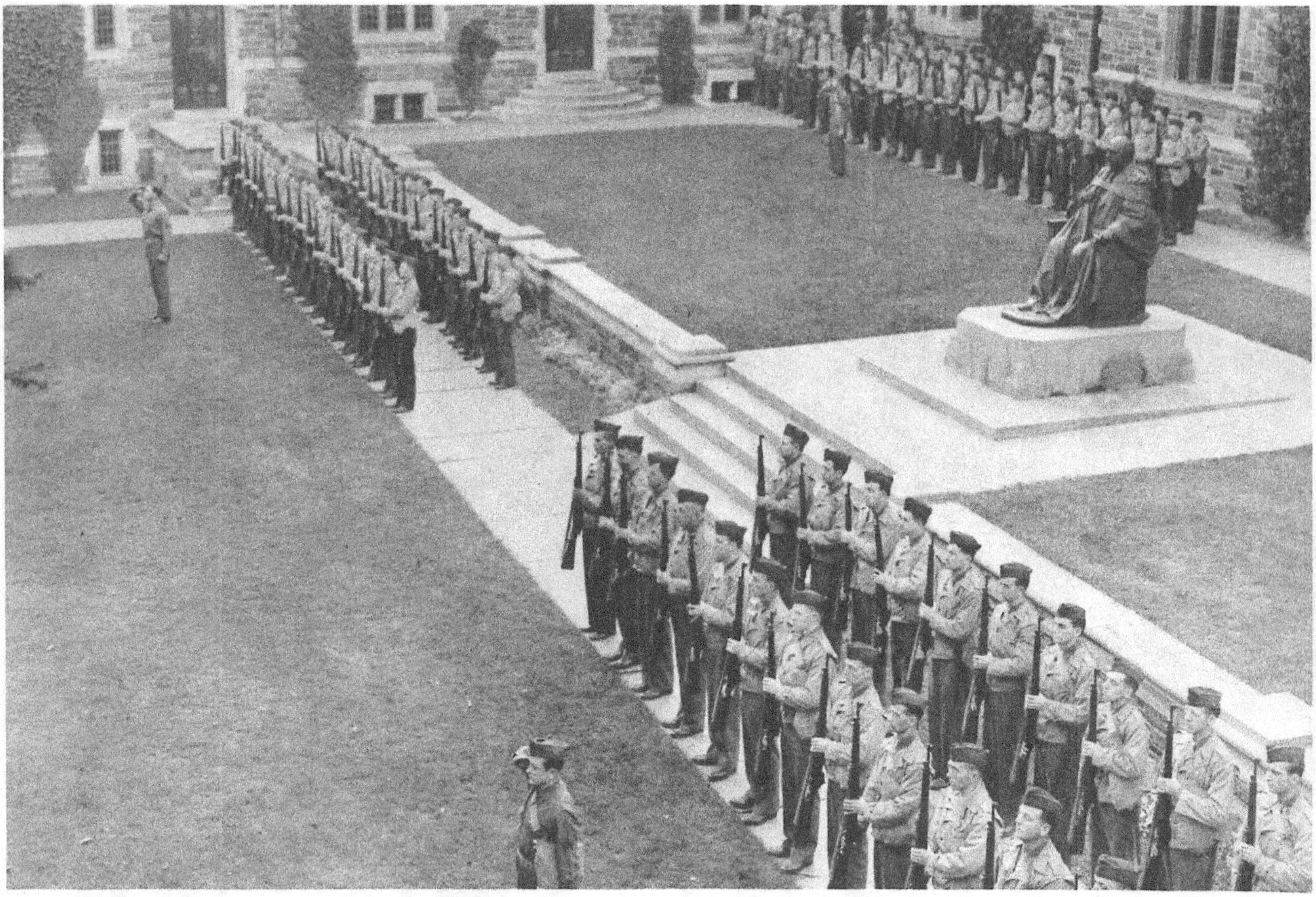

PHOTO BY MENZIES

THE ARMY POST EXCHANGE SCHOOL, at the Graduate College. Two thousand men and women passed through this School, in the early days of the war. As in World War I, the Graduate College took on a military character, but its academic appearance was not entirely lost. The University trained some 20,000 men, including undergraduates and those in special schools.

PHOTO BY MENZIES

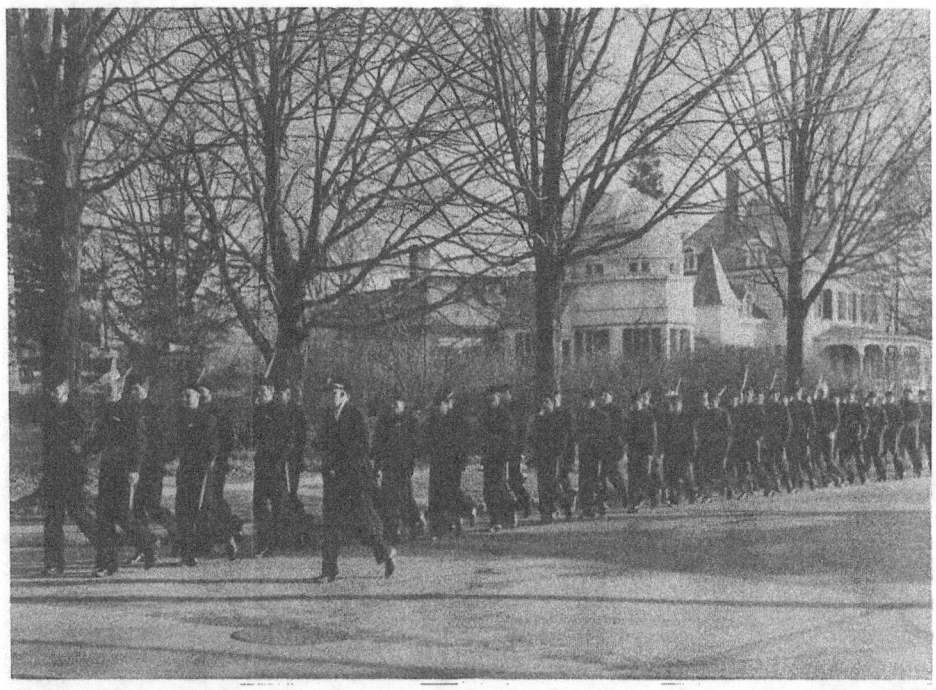

MARCHING TO CLASS. A Navy unit shows the effects of long drill hours as it marches up Prospect Avenue, on the way to lecture hall in McCosh.

PHOTO BY MENZIES

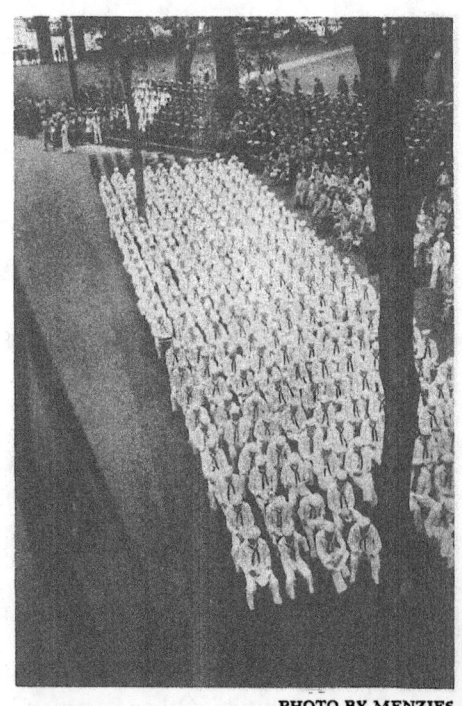

WARTIME COMMENCEMENT. Navy officers and enlisted men, at graduation.

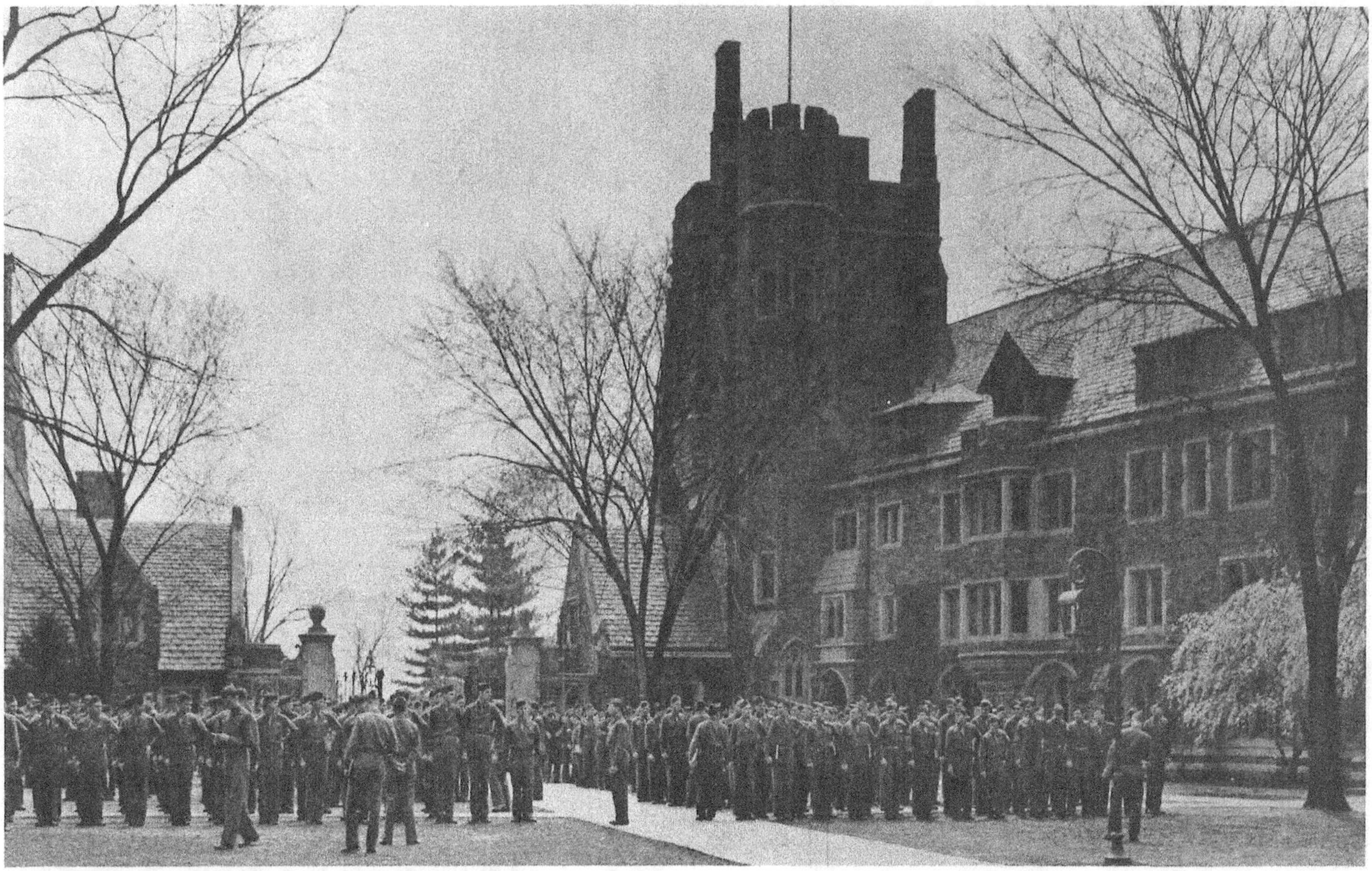

PHOTO BY MENZIES

FALL IN! During World War II, the campus presented an unusual spectacle of activity at six in the morning.

PHOTO BY MENZIES

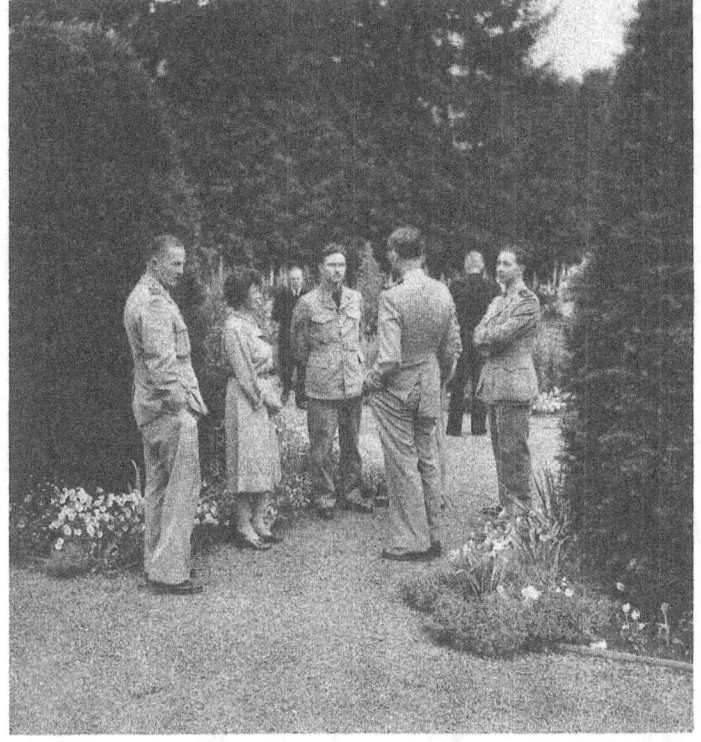

BRITISH INDOCTRINATION. During the war, groups of British and Dominion officers and men were brought to Princeton for weekends, in which the mores of American life were explained by lecture, conference, and observation. Here Mrs. Dodds entertains a visiting group at Prospect.

PHOTO BY MENZIES

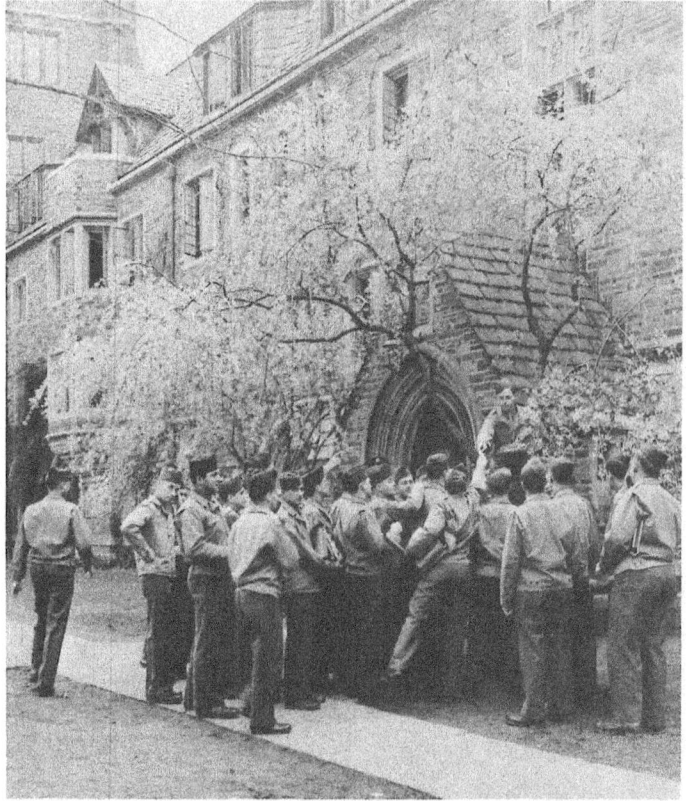

MAIL TIME IN SPRING. The most popular member of the Army Specialized Training Program hands out mail to his fellow service men, in front of 1904–Henry Hall.

PRINCETON'S SCIENTISTS played an all-important role in the development of the atomic bomb. In the top picture three physicists examine a piece of "jade" from the melted sand at Alamogordo. From left to right are Professors Henry D. Smyth 1918, author of the Smyth Report; John A. Wheeler, who helped formulate the Bohr-Wheeler theory of nuclear fission; and Eugene P. Wigner, whose most significant work was done in the theory of chain reactors.

ATOMIC ENERGY was the subject of the first "Preceptorial of the Air," in a series of broadcasts in 1945. As shown in the picture below, the participants were, from left to right: Professor Smyth; Professor N. Howell Furman, who headed the Princeton group of analytical chemists; Professor Roy D. Welch, who presided over each "preceptorial"; Professor Hugh S. Taylor, who directed the Princeton group of physical chemists; and Professor Harold H. Sprout, expert in naval strategy.

Two Wartime Research Projects. The measurement of pressures caused by different kinds of fills was a project carried out for the Navy Department by Professor Gregory T. Tschebotarioff of the Department of Civil Engineering. A large steel tank with flexible sheets was built under the stadium, and the pressures obtaining at different levels were found by delicate recording apparatus. Above, Professor Tschebotarioff (left) and his assistant, Edward R. Ward, record a series of measurements. The tank was filled countless times with different kinds of earth to provide accurate and complete data.

War research in the study of air streams traveling at supersonic speeds was an important project conducted for the Navy in Palmer Physical Laboratory. Light rays, rather than mechanical devices, were used as a means of measurement. The project was carried out by Professor Rudolf W. Ladenburg, shown in the accompanying picture (at the right), and his associates Dr. John R. Winckler (center) and Dr. Cletus C. Van Voorhis.

COURSE IN PHOTOGRAMMETRY. Princeton gave many special courses in World War II. Here Professor Philip Kissam 1919 of the Department of Civil Engineering instructs two students in an extension course given in 1942, in the Engineering, Science and Management War Training Program.

THE MATERIALS TESTING LABORATORY (left) of the Department of Civil Engineering was used to test soil samples in order to find the best pavements for airports. This research project, carried out for the Civil Areonautics Administration, was under the charge of Professor Gregory T. Tschebotarioff. The steel supporting frame had earlier been used by Professor George E. Beggs for structural tests of models of the towers of the Golden Gate Bridge.

THE FOURTH *Princeton*. Since 1844 when Robert F. Stockton 1813 built the first *Princeton*, the Navy has usually had a ship of this name in service. The fourth *Princeton* was a carrier of 10,000 tons, christened at her launching in Camden by Mrs. Dodds, in 1942.

This ship saw more active service than her three predecessors and her successor. For two years she was engaged in warfare in the Pacific, taking part in innumerable strikes at the enemy. In October 1944 she was hit by landbased Japanese planes east of Luzon, in the Second Battle of the Philippine Sea. Firefighting efforts, both by her crew and by other warships in the vicinity, proved unavailing, and the order was then given to abandon ship. She was then sunk by U. S. gunfire. Nearly all her complement of 1,300 officers and men was saved.

This picture shows the cruiser *Birmingham* alongside hopelessly attempting to put out the fire.

Following her loss the fifth *Princeton*, a carrier of 27,000 tons, was commissioned in Philadelphia.

Undergraduate Life

Princeton, like the older liberal arts colleges of America, was based upon the residential principle; it early accepted the idea that the college was itself "a society in which the student was to practice and thus to learn the art of living the good life with his fellows and his elders." Its spirit has essentially been democratic. Indeed for over a century undergraduate life was marked by a Spartan simplicity; the legend that part of the town's colored population is descended from slaves brought as attendants by southern students is nonsense. In the modern period about one-third of the student body has supported itself in whole or in part, while the University annually distributes a quarter of a million dollars in scholarships and loans. Only in reference to the upperclass eating clubs have there been charges that Princeton has departed from its democratic tradition. Today campus democracy finds expression in self-government through the Undergraduate Council, while student publications have traditionally been free of censorship from the faculty.

The fact that the town of Princeton has always been quite rural has had its effect upon student life. The enormous acreage possessed by the University has permitted an orderly expansion of the campus, and the English park-like landscaping, in effect since the days of McCosh, is perfectly adapted to the gently rolling terrain. Yet every building is within easy walking distance; one does not take a trolley to reach tennis courts or playing fields. The general effect has been to promote an outdoor life, to stimulate interest in sports, and to make popular the University's policy of "Athletics for all." Another result, no less important, has been to further that communal feeling so essential to undergraduate spirit.

As in all old institutions, activities and customs and traditions have changed throughout the years. For nearly a century and a half extra-curricular activity centered around the two Halls, Cliosophic and Whig; but as interest in debating diminished and as eating clubs gained priority in loyalty, the Halls have lost their general appeal. Today, outside of athletics, the various publications and the Triangle Club rate first in student popularity; the last, with its extensive trips, has become an all-important social organization.

The two moving picture theaters have had their effects during the past three decades. Spending the evening with song and beer has declined in favor, despite the new Nassau Tavern; and the old grad of the 1890's misses the fervor of the songs and the class spirit of his student days. The lessening of class spirit has been expressed, too, in the disappearance of class rushes and parades, and in the wartime removal of the freshman dink.

Today the undergraduate is more serious in his activities. The four-course plan with its emphasis upon independent work takes more of his time, and weekending is less frequent than twenty years ago. The Student Christian Association carries on the task of the old Philadelphian Society, and new organizations, such as The Print Club, have sprung up to foster cultural interests. Today the post-war undergraduate is fully conscious of living in a changing world, and he is not indifferent to his responsibilities in the future.

Curricular

> **FINAL EXAMINATION.**
> **1841.**
> **BELLES-LETTRES.**
>
> *Note.* The answers may be as brief as is compatible with correctness.
>
> 1. What is meant by Belles-Lettres? 2. What is Rhetoric? 3. What is Criticism? 4. What is Style?
>
> 5. Explain the terms *Purity*, *Propriety*, and *Precision*, as used by Blair. 6. What is meant by a *loose style*? 7. What are *synonymous words*?
>
> 8. What four properties are most essential to a perfect sentence? 9. What rules must be observed, in order to the *unity* of a sentence?
>
> 10. Enumerate Blair's divisions of style, in regard to ornament, the *Dry*, &c.
>
> 11. Name the six parts that compose a regular formal oration. 12. What are the three ends, to one or other of which an *Introduction* should be subservient? 13. What are the material rules for a *Division*?

AN EXAMINATION IN BELLES LETTRES, 1841. Examinations were entirely oral until the 1830's, when written examinations were introduced. An eighteenth century student recorded that in his day examinations were taken in the morning in full dress—"we all march in like so many criminals, the Faculty take their seats formally and we extend in a great circle around the room, 26 of us." This course examination was given by James W. Alexander, professor of belles lettres.

COLLEGE OF NEW JERSEY
Examination of the Senior Class in Astronomy, August 9,
1841

1. What is the form of the earth? How is it ascertained? What is the dip of the horizon,—and to what is this dip equal?
2. Describe the apparent diurnal revolution of the heavens, as seen by,
    (1.) A spectator at the equator;—
    (2.) At one of the poles;—
    (3.) At some intermediate position.
Also, state in what respect the apparent motion as seen in the southern hemisphere, would differ from that observed in the northern.
3. Describe the various phenomena dependant upon the refraction of the Earth's atmosphere. Account for the blue colour of remote objects.
4. What is the *siderial*, and what the *tropical* year;—and why is the one longer than the other?
5. What seems to be the physical constitution of the substances which surround the sun;—and what are the phenomena whereby such constitution is indicated?
6. Why is not noon, in general, the warmest period of the day, and June, in our hemisphere, the hottest month in the year?
7. What is the form of the shadows of the Earth and Moon;—and why have they such a form? What are the distinctions between the umbra and penumbra?
8. State the causes of solar and lunar eclipses. When and where do they occur? When are they partial, and when total? Under what circumstances will an eclipse of the Sun be annular? Why do not eclipses occur every month?
9. In what respects do the four minor planets differ from the Earth and others of the same order? Is there any theory which attempts to account for these peculiarities?
10. State some of the peculiarities in the physical constitution of comets. What proves that they shine by reflected light? Have the orbits of any been essentially changed? Who first predicted the return of a comet?
11. Describe the appearance, connexion, and motions of double stars.
12. What appears to be the constitution of the milky way? Has anything else been discovered, having an apparently similar constitution? How do the fixed stars seem to be distributed and arranged.

AN EXAMINATION IN ASTRONOMY, 1841. An early examination by Stephen Alexander, professor of mathematics and astronomy in the mid-nineteenth century.

EXAMINATION IN JURISPRUDENCE.
25 January, 1902.

1. Give a full explanation, with illustrations, of what is meant by the statement that "law is an organic product". Explain also by what characteristics of the life of men in society law is produced.
2. Illustrate the same subject still further by defining *Jural Relationships* and analyzing the method of their origin and development.
3. What part does the systematic study of Jurisprudence (that is, Legal Science) play in the development of law? At what stage of the growth of law is it apt to play its part most influentially?
4. Explain how each of the following, in turn, plays the part of an "Originative and Participant Factor" in the growth of law: The *Family*, the *Church*, *Orders and Classes*, the *Corporation*, the *Local Community* or *Commune*, the *Province*, the *State*, the *Society of States*.
5. What is at present the chief and almost only way in which law is originated? What forms of origination preceded this, and why did they disappear or fall into the background?
6. What are the several subdivisions of Private Law? What are "rights *in rem*"? What are "rights *in personam*"? Under which of these do the rights of property fall? Define "Ownership", and analyze the definition sufficiently to point out just what it means.
7. What does Sir Frederick Pollock say of "Things" as the subject-matter of rights? How wide is the meaning of the word, and what several sorts of objects does it include?
8. Give illustrations (out of Pollock) of the extension of the principle of ownership to *incorporeal* things, and show how far like, and how far unlike, the ownership of incorporeal things is to the ownership of corporeal things.
9. Upon what principle did "negotiable instruments" become negotiable? What characteristics must a contract to pay money have to get full negotiability and make credit "currency in law as well as in fact"?
10. What is meant by "Custom" in English law? What are the conditions of its validity?

AN EXAMINATION IN JURISPRUDENCE, 1902. Woodrow Wilson's courses in constitutional law and jurisprudence were among the most popular of his period.

PRINCETON UNIVERSITY
DEPARTMENT OF HISTORY
SENIOR COMPREHENSIVE EXAMINATION
THE GENERAL EXAMINATION

May 15, 1943   Time: 4 hours

NOTICE

At the request of the Student Honor Committee, no smoking is to be permitted in examination rooms, and examinations are to be conducted only in rooms regularly scheduled for the examination, or arranged for by the instructor in charge of the examination.

Answer each question in a separate book, marking the number of the question and your own examination number clearly on the outside of each book.

Answer *two* questions.

1. The French are fond of saying that their country has been the center of European civilization from the time of Charlemagne to the present. Give arguments for and against this assertion.

2. "The history of western civilization from the Roman Empire to the World War was characterized among other things by the growth of individual freedom. Men of thought have increasingly trumpeted the gospel of liberty, and men of action have succeeded more and more in putting that gospel into action." Comment on this statement, justifying your remarks and arguments with illustrative detail.

3. Discuss the origins of the political ideas dominant in the United States from the Declaration of Independence to the Civil War. How far were they based on English experience, on writings of continental scholars, on the American physical and intellectual environment?

4. "The Catholic Church played an essentially negative and conservative rôle during the period 1500-1815. It was no longer trying to guide European society; it was merely trying to keep alive." Discuss.

5. In both the fifteenth and the eighteenth centuries established institutions and beliefs were crumbling under the impact of new forces. Compare and contrast the new ideas and forms of behavior which were responsible for the violent changes which took place at the end of each century.

PART OF A HISTORY COMPREHENSIVE EXAMINATION, 1943. With the introduction of the four-course plan, beginning with the Class of 1925, long junior and senior comprehensive examinations were inaugurated to test the student in his general grasp of his field. The questions are so devised as to test not merely the student's knowledge of facts but, more important, his powers of analysis.

Since 1893 the HONOR SYSTEM has been one of the most cherished and successful features of Princeton education. The pledge is written on every examination.

When the system was established, it brought all kinds of friendly comment from the New York press, which wondered at first at its effectiveness. *Harper's Weekly* was impressed with the informality with which examinations were conducted, and its artist here depicts a professor vainly trying to collar an itinerant dog while a student is engaged in the common pastime of borrowing a pencil. (From the issue of June 1, 1895.)

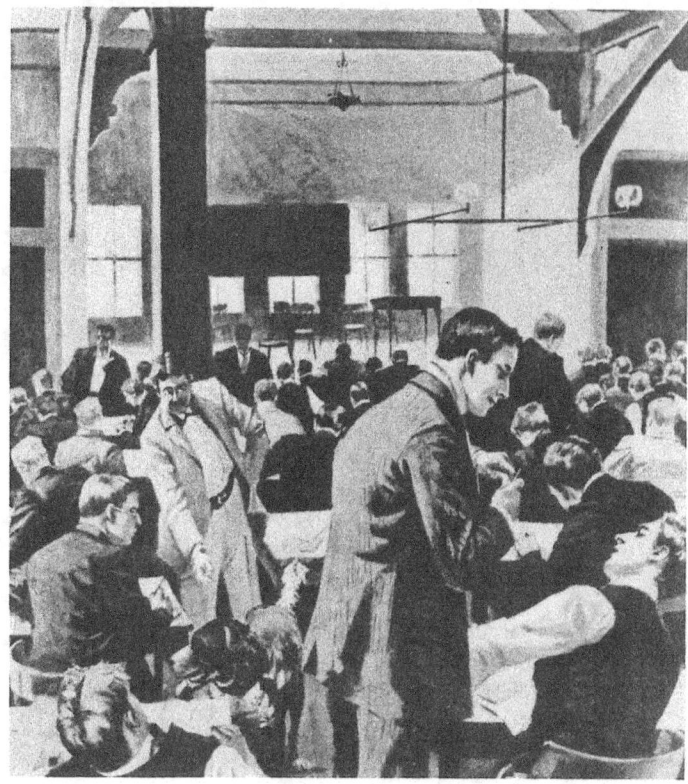

A LECTURE IN EUROPEAN HISTORY. The lecture system goes back to Witherspoon's day, but probably no professor has been as consistently popular as Walter P. Hall who is here expounding the French Revolution, in the Frick auditorium. This scene (opposite) was taken at the close of World War II.

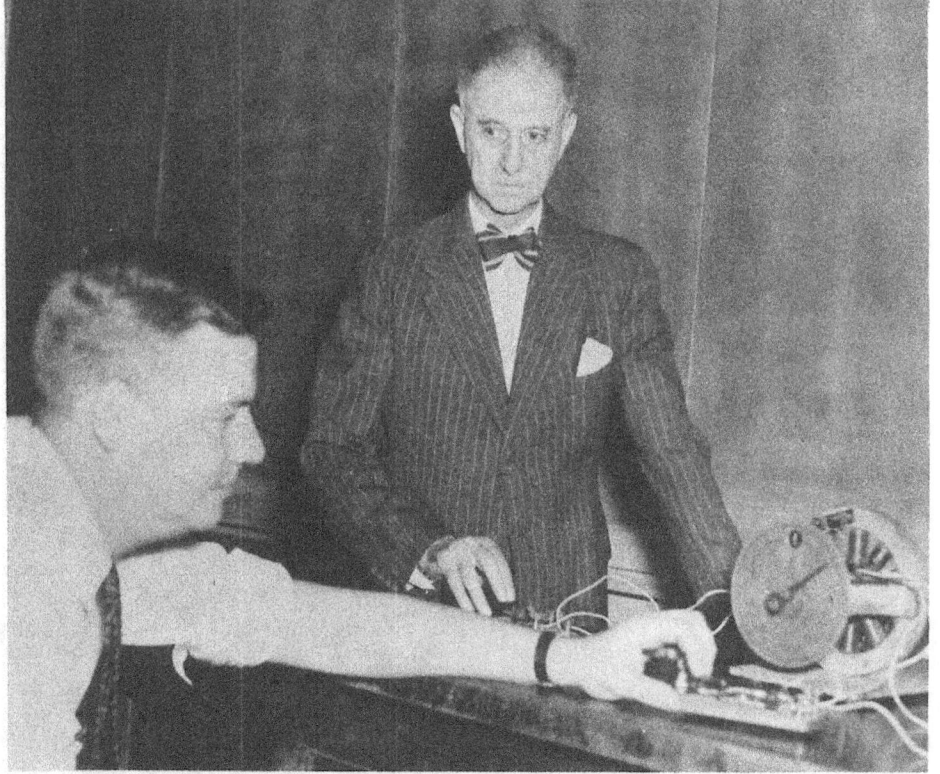

UPPERCLASS PRECEPTORIAL. Inaugurated in 1905, the preceptorial system marked a major advance in American educational methods. It has been widely followed in other universities.

Here a preceptorial conference is conducted by Professor Thomas J. Wertenbaker, in his famous course in Colonial Civilization. The dean of colonial historians today, Professor Wertenbaker was also the Bicentennial Historian of the University.

CLASSROOM DEMONSTRATION. Professor Herbert S. Langfeld, recently retired chairman of the Psychology Department, is justly famous for his lectures in Psychology 101. Here he demonstrates, on a more or less willing subject, the use of the Dunlap Chronoscope to measure the speed of reaction.

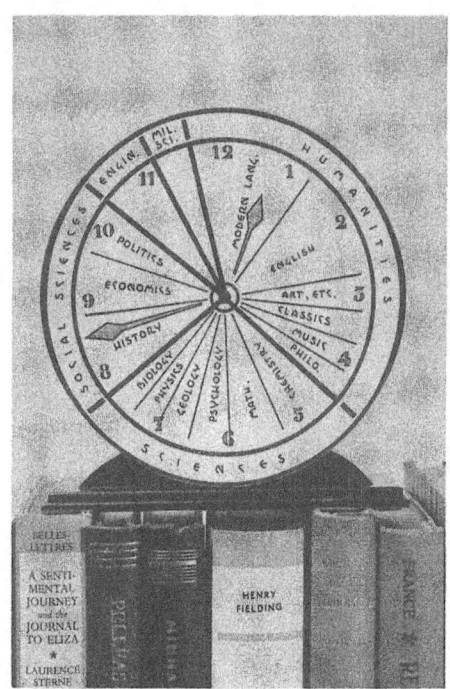

Modern Course Enrollment. Music and religion have appeared and classics have declined, in the modern era. This graph indicates the popularity of different subjects in 1939.

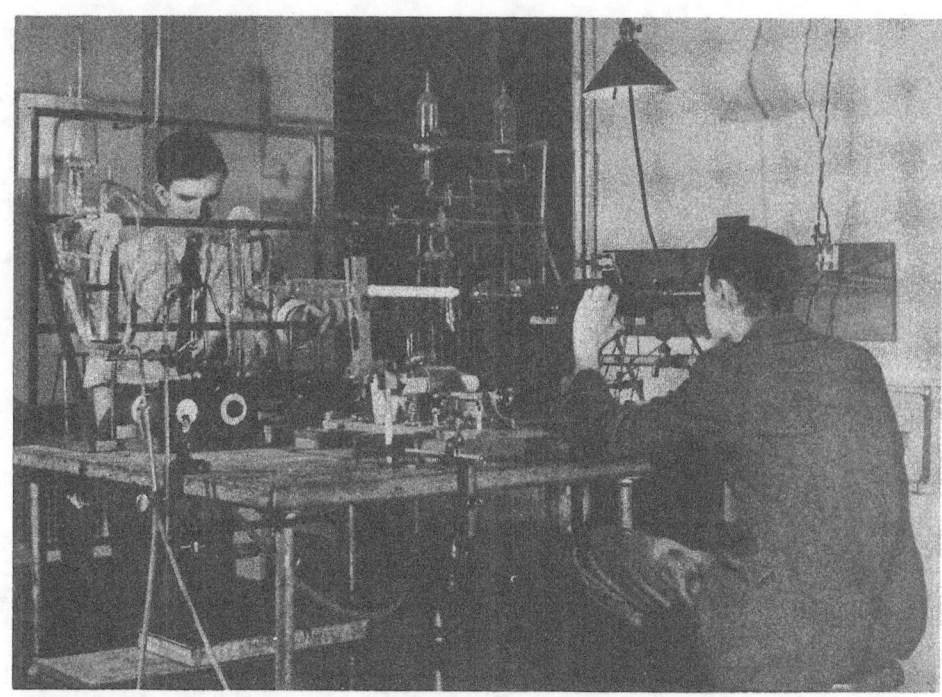

In Palmer Physical Laboratory. Thesis work keeps every senior busy. The four-course plan requires each senior to do individual work on some subject or project of his own choice, within the departmental field.

Work in the Library stacks is encouraged as one of the best means of getting the upperclass student acquainted with his source material.

Deadline for Senior Thesis. Senior theses have to be turned in by spring of senior year. Those who get a head start on the project are the happiest. Some theses of outstanding quality have been published.

THE ENGINE LABORATORY. The School of Engineering is justly proud of its laboratories, which are constantly acquiring new equipment. Here, in the Engine Laboratory, undergraduates are watching the indicators.

A CLASS IN MODELING. The Creative Arts Program was inaugrated in 1939 to provide opportunities for students showing particular aptitude in painting, sculpture, music, and writing. Professor Joseph Brown, who also acts as boxing instructor on the side, teaches a small but serious group of undergraduates.

NOT ALL WORK IS INDOORS. Activities of prospective architects are usually confined to McCormick Hall, but occasionally the draughtsmen venture forth to consider a practical problem on the campus. Here a group of local urchins is attracted to an unaccustomed activity in front of Nassau Hall.

The School of Architecture has achieved an enviable reputation, and many students in this section of the Department of Art and Archaeology remain to do graduate work preparatory to entering the architectural profession.

SURVEYING THE CAMPUS. Incipient engineers survey the campus again and again, but the results rarely vary. Surveyors prefer spring days for their operations, but sometimes it can be too warm.

AN INVESTIGATION OF ANTHRACITE. Students in the School of Public and International Affairs sometimes take field trips to study political and economic problems at first hand. Here a group is equipped to enter a mine at Wilkes-Barre, Pennsylvania.

ELEMENTS OF FOREIGN POLICY. By simulation of actual procedures in the outside world, students receive valuable training in the School of Public and International Affairs. This Conference in 1946 is examining the policies of the great powers in southeastern Europe. The "British Ambassador," G. L. Regard 1944, expounds his country's aims.

SUMMER FIELD WORK IN GEOLOGY, 1930. Each summer the students in geology make an extended trip to the West. Here the undergraduates and faculty are grouped around the entrance to a coal mine at Red Lodge, Montana.

INSPECTING A GLACIER, 1941. A group of interested undergraduates, in the Summer School of Geology and Natural Resources, examines Grinnell Glacier in Montana, at close range.

PHOTO BY MENZIES

TERM'S END. The end of each term sees the posting of grades in Nassau Hall. These two undergraduates show an unusual composure in viewing the results.

Customs and Traditions

A STUDENT'S ROOM, 1845. The changing mores of undergraduate life are perhaps best reflected in the appearance of students' rooms. Until 1838 students arrived in Princeton by stage coach, and their baggage was necessarily limited. But even after the railroad was laid out on the south bank of the canal, most room furnishings continued to be handed down from one class to the other, as indeed they are at the present. The campus today still boasts of furniture that has done stalwart service for generations of Princetonians.

This sketch is the first portrayal of a student's room that we have; it was probably in Nassau Hall. At this time candles had replaced the earlier lard lamps.

A ROOM IN THE LATE 1870's. This room (below) is typical of the era of gaslight, and of athletic and hunting equipment nailed to the walls. This is 9 North West College, when it was occupied by Arthur H. Scribner 1881.

DÉCOR, IN THE 1880's. The room of L. Rodman Wanamaker 1886, at 12 East Witherspoon, was considered the height of luxuriousness in undergraduate quarters. The high hat and cane lent a note of studied elegance.

SIXTY-FIVE YEARS LATER. 9 North West College in 1943. The old order changeth, giving way to the new—except for the crack in the door.

THE HAZERS HAZED, OR A FRESHMAN'S REVENGE. The custom of hazing was almost as old as Nassau Hall itself, the official "Account" of 1764 stating that the students of that day gave and received "tokens of respect and subjection." Most freshmen bore up under the ordeal but occasionally one rebelled. In 1878 a freshman named Line, after being severely hazed by A. H. Atterbury and J. B. Carter of the Class of 1880, captured the two offenders and, with the aid of a few classmates, shaved their heads and paddled them until they were a mass of bruises. On being freed, the two sophomores armed themselves and in an exchange of shots Atterbury was wounded. The incident was widely reported and the *Police Gazette*, of March 2, 1878, hastened to present its version of the "barbaric custom."

SOPHOMORE PROCLAMATION. The last decades of the nineteenth century saw an intense class rivalry between freshmen and sophomores, and the proclamations of each class covered all the barns and freight cars in the vicinity. This sophomore proclamation (upper left) had the right tone of condescension.

SOPHOMORES HAVING FUN. A verdant freshman being compelled to scrub his feet on the pretext that they smelled—or maybe they did.

HORSING WAS MILD. A freshman entertaining a group of sophomores with some forced vocal efforts. (From *Harper's Weekly*, October 21, 1899.)

ORREN JACK TURNER

FLOUR PICTURE. Until the late 1920's, freshmen had to endure a barrage of flour bombs and rotten fruit before their class picture could be taken. Here a freshman class, daubed but unbowed, poses as nonchalantly as possible on the steps of Whig Hall.

ROSE AND SON

SOPHOMORES' DELIGHT. Some luckless freshmen, with coats inside out, are horsed by sophomores by being forced to climb into a room in Hamilton Hall. Horsing officially came to an end in 1914, but from time to time sophomores have continued to harass bumptious freshmen. When horsing, the sophomores often wore "horsing hats," hence the berets.

AN EARLY CANE SPREE. In its earliest days the cane spree literally constituted a class struggle between the freshmen and sophomores. Later, each class selected its champions in the different weight groups. Opinion varied as to whether the inside or the outside grip gave one an advantage. (From *Scribner's*, March 1877.)

STEALING THE CLAPPER. Stealing the clapper from the bell in Nassau Hall has from time immemorial been a challenge to freshmen. At the upper left, *Scribner's* of June 1897 depicts a freshman making the climb; while at the left, two members of 1894, G. Howard Bright and Louis I. Reichner, proudly hold their trophy.

CLOSE DECISION IN THE CANE SPREE. The cane spree, one of Princeton's oldest customs, came down to World War II, and may well be revived. Two modern boneless champions exhibit their prowess.

CLASS SPIRIT, CAUSE AND EFFECT. Three freshmen of the Class of 1895 reveal the accuracy of the sophomore fusillade in a snow fight.
Left to right: Darwin R. James, Jr.; John P. Poe; and Arthur L. Wheeler.

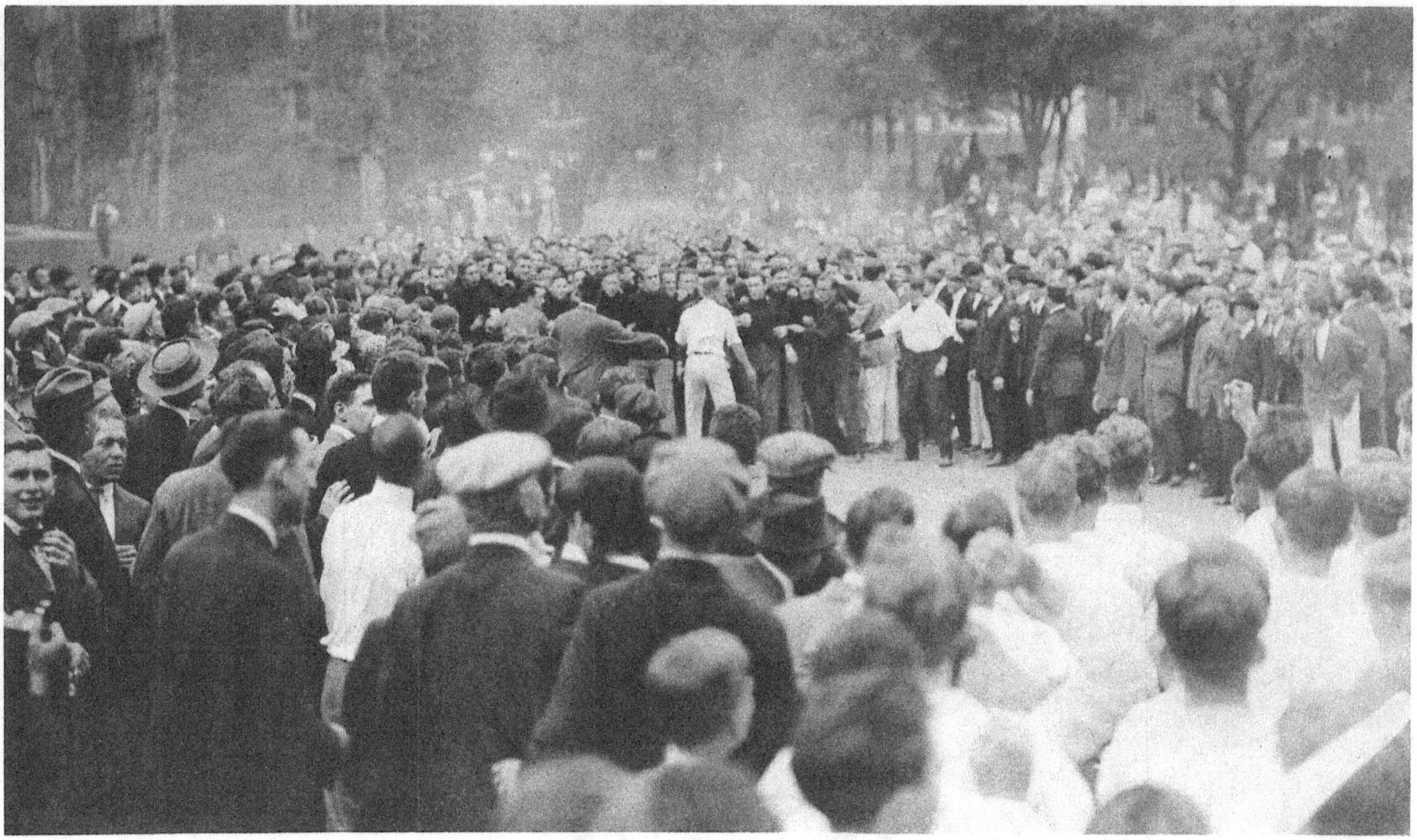

ROSE AND SON

PREPARING FOR THE CLASS RUSH. For forty years the class rush between freshmen and sophomores was one of the major events of the fall term. The latter tried to prevent the freshmen from holding their election of officers. Here the freshmen in black sweaters are coached by the juniors, while the sophomores in white bar the entrance to the Gym.

THE TWO CLASSES CLASH. The *mêlée at its height, in* 1913. All are so closely packed that not much damage is done.

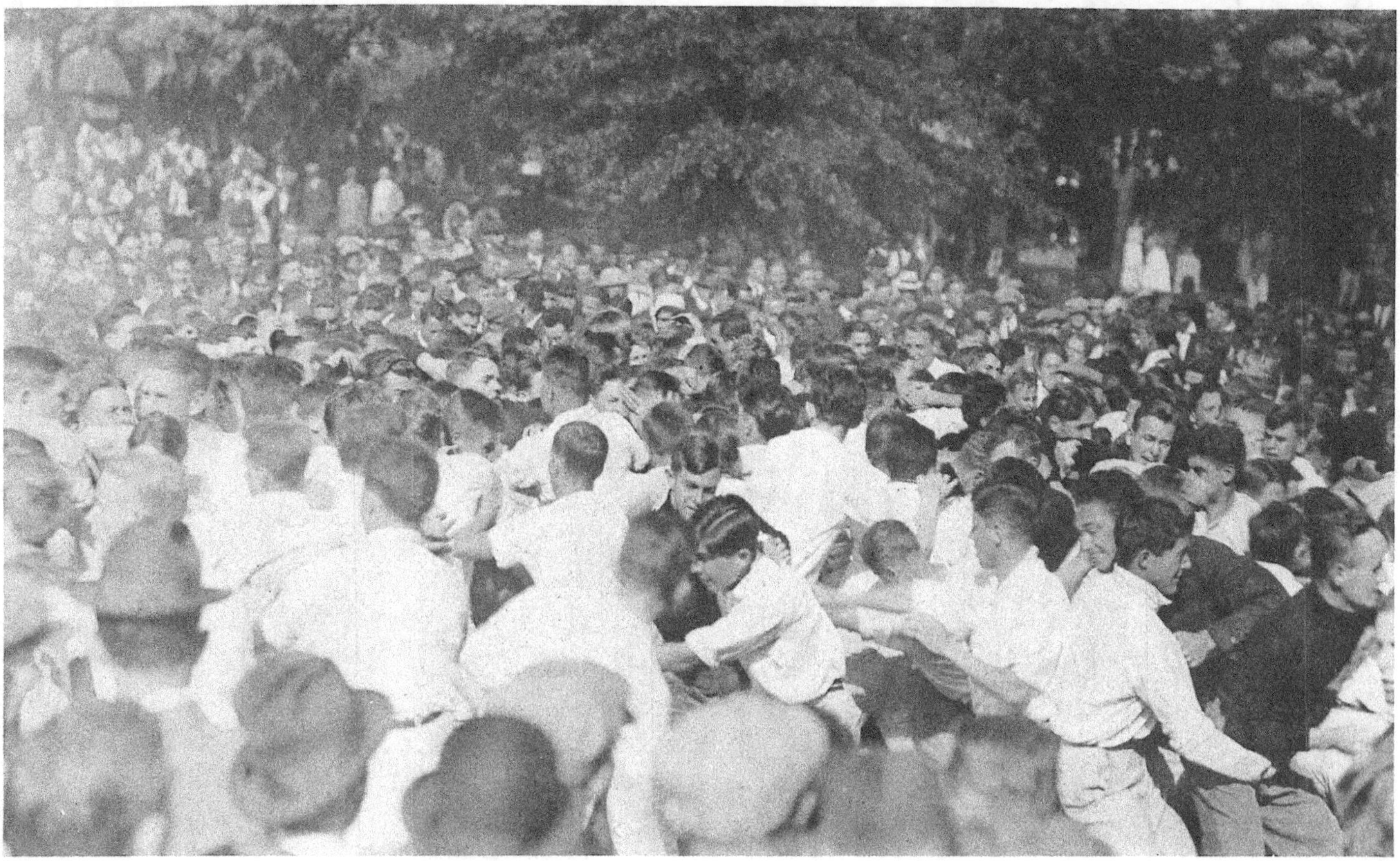

ROSE AND SON

END OF AN ERA. The last class rush came in 1915. Here the irresistible column of 1919 smacks the immovable mass of 1918, in front of the Gymnasium. Because of the death of a student in this rush, the hoary institution came to an end by official decree, and the flour picture became a less strenuous substitute. The Cannon rush, in which the freshmen tried to reach the Cannon guarded by sophomores, also disappeared.

ROSE AND SON

RATTLING THE PITCHER. For many years the fall baseball game between freshmen and sophomores was an important event that fostered class spirit. Here the Class of 1908 blows lustily on tin horns in an attempt to disconcert the enemy, but the score was 1 to 1.

FIRST TOUCH OF WINTER. Organized snow fights have long since disappeared under the faculty ban; but impromptu engagements sometimes spring up. Today there are no physical encounters between freshmen and their mortal enemies, the sophomores.

VACATION IN PRINCETON. Travel was so slow, before the Civil War, that many students remained in Princeton during vacations. This drawing, by an undergraduate in 1845, gives proof, if any were needed, that students spent their spare time in much the same pursuits as at present.

THE WELL DRESSED UNDERGRADUATE, IN 1860. In recent years various men's clothing stores have attempted to emphasize Princeton as a style center. Here in 1860 the newest fashions are shown in the window of McVeigh's Tailor Shop on Nassau Street; and this pose was apparently made to indicate that the Princeton student was thoroughly *au courant* with the latest styles. The youth on the left with the elk's tooth would seem to have caught the spirit.

SKYLARKING IN THE 1860's. A group of undergraduates having fun with a skeleton. But the rather solemn looks belie any great amount of excitement. At that time the little village of Princeton afforded slight opportunity for entertainment.

The Famous Class of 1879, in its Freshman Year.

Town versus Gown. Since the days of Samuel Stanhope Smith Princeton has "enjoyed" a reputation for riots caused by undergraduates. In the late nineteenth century feeling between the town and gown was occasionally manifested by snow fights and fist fights. In 1883 a riot started over the sale of patent medicine by a passing vendor. Apparently the students didn't want any, and the townspeople did. (From the *Police Gazette* of November 3, 1883.)

wnee Bill's Circus. Students routed cowboys and Indians pitched battle. (From the *Police Gazette* of June 3, 1899.)

Student Riot in the Town. This one, in the 1880's, occurred when the undergraduates broke up a lecture by a hypnotist.

AN EVENING'S ENTERTAINMENT. The movies have been in Princeton for some forty years and have had their effect on student life. No more do undergraduates gather in the old Princeton Inn or the "Nass" to while away the evening with song, as they did in the 'nineties. Dad Struve's Arcade was long a popular place for an evening's entertainment, but these students were apparently not too pleased with *Such a Little Queen*, Famous Players' hit of 1914. The old Arcade has become a bowling alley, and the Garden and the new Playhouse accommodate the present crowds.

Poler's Recess developed out of the old Horn Spree, "invented" by the Class of 1858. On a moment's notice, students would start blowing horns at night until caught by the outraged faculty. Poler's Recess, coming at nine in the evening during the exam period, let everyone blow off steam for five minutes, after which everyone went back to work, theoretically. Poler's Recess was revived after the interruption of World War I, and it may again make the night suddenly hideous with noise.

At the upper left, four polers in 34 University Hall are hard at work. The reader will observe the pin-up girls of 1915. Above, Poler's Recess is at its peak. Curiously enough no one was ever hit by the bullets ricocheting about the campus. And left, the polers are exhausted by their efforts.

FESTIVITIES FOR ST. PATRICK. The St. Patrick's Day Parade permitted the seniors to have some fun before settling down on the home stretch of the spring term. The floats in the Parade of 1915 featured Dean McClenahan's trip to Europe.

JUNIOR HI-HAT PARADE. In the days before World War I, one of the principal events of early June was the Junior Hi-Hat Parade, when juniors could don high hats for the first time and proudly marched through the town.

ROSE AND SON

THE ST. PATRICK'S DAY PARADE grew out of the senior parade at the freshman-sophomore baseball game. The custom came to an end at World War I. The Parade usually concluded with seniors haranguing the crowd from the balcony of the ancient Nassau Inn. Even a late spring put no damper on the general enthusiasm of this group.

The long line of proctors is headed by MATTHEW GOLDIE who flourished in the days of McCosh. He rounded up erring students, suppressed riots, and maintained classroom discipline.

JOHNNY DEGNAN was the campus policeman in the gay nineties. He is flanked by DENNY SULLIVAN, the college messenger. "Johnny, Johnny Degnan, do you want me?" was a familiar refrain.

JOHN W. TOPLEY was the head proctor at the end of the century. In 1907 he set up a saloon on Nassau Street, to the dismay of the faculty. This rare view shows him at his bar.

Universally called "Bill Coons" for some unaccountable reason, WILLIAM COAN succeeded Topley in 1907. His huge bulk was no handicap to him in his amazing sleuthing career.

After Coan retired in 1918 to become fire chief in the town, Dean McClenahan offered the position of head proctor to Henry H. (Hank) Bovie. The latter accepted and worked closely with "Dean Mac," and many a graduate owes his diploma to this combination. The Dean used to send Bovie to the rooms of students deficient in their studies, and as a result many of them concentrated on their work and graduated. After graduation, they would ask Bovie to affix his signature to their diplomas.

Today Bovie, who left the proctor's office in 1926, heads the detectives on the Borough's force. His hardest night's work as a proctor came after the Dean abolished student automobiles, and the undergraduates organized an automobile parade in violent protest.

Head proctor since 1926 has been Francis X. (Frank) Hogarty. In his experience the prohibition era was the most exciting, and the last important riot followed the cane spree of 1930. Frank is here setting out on a serious mission.

This scene, posed to reveal the sleuth-like tactics of Proctor Michael C. Kopliner, shows him uncovering an alleged political meeting on the campus in 1934. Sitting on the beer keg is Edward F. Prichard, Jr., 1935, leading Democrat.

Of the campus characters who long made Princeton the scene of their operations, first place goes to JIMMY JOHNSON. Escaping from slavery before the Civil War and then being apprehended in Princeton by his owner, he was purchased through funds raised in part by the student body. For some forty years he wandered daily over the campus with his basket of fruit and candy. In his late years, he took an assistant named Spader; and the latter in turn was succeeded by Jigger, who carries on at present.

Campus Activities

Student Employment. The University has always had a large percentage of students who earn their expenses in whole or in part. The BUREAU OF STUDENT AID AND EMPLOYMENT acts as a clearing house for the various activities. Waiting on table in Commons is the most popular pursuit for underclassmen, but a hundred and one other opportunities are available. The pictures below show a few of these activities.

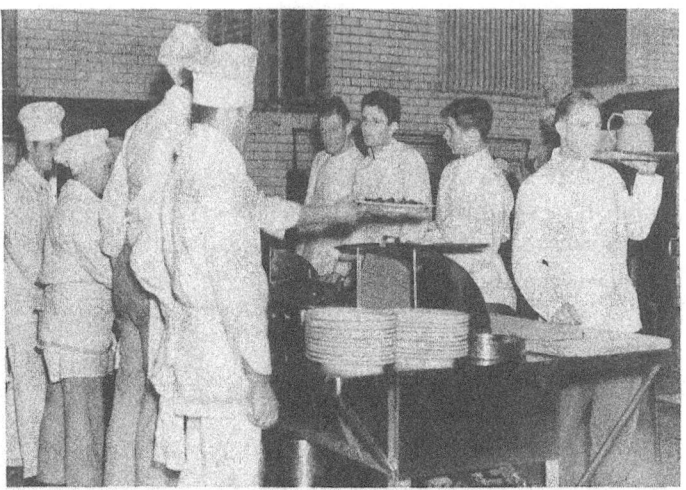

Student Waiters at the Serving Table in Commons

The Sandwichman Is Always a Popular Caller at Night

Brawn Counts with the Students' Express Service

Running the Travel Bureau Is Next Best to Going Yourself

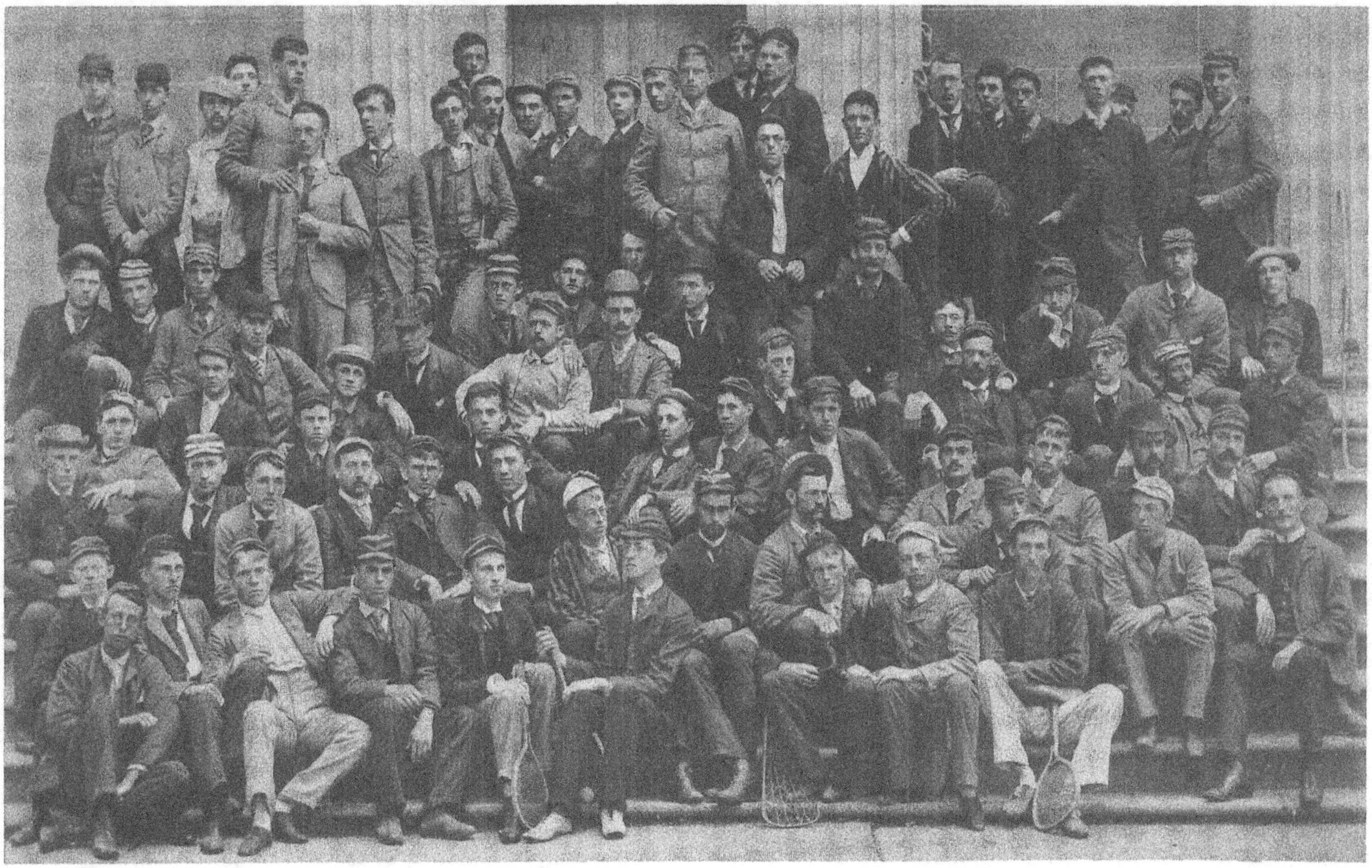

CULVER SERVICE

Members of CLIO, in 1889. For nearly two centuries the Cliosophic and American Whig Societies have been an integral part of student life, and during the first century these debating and literary clubs were all-important.

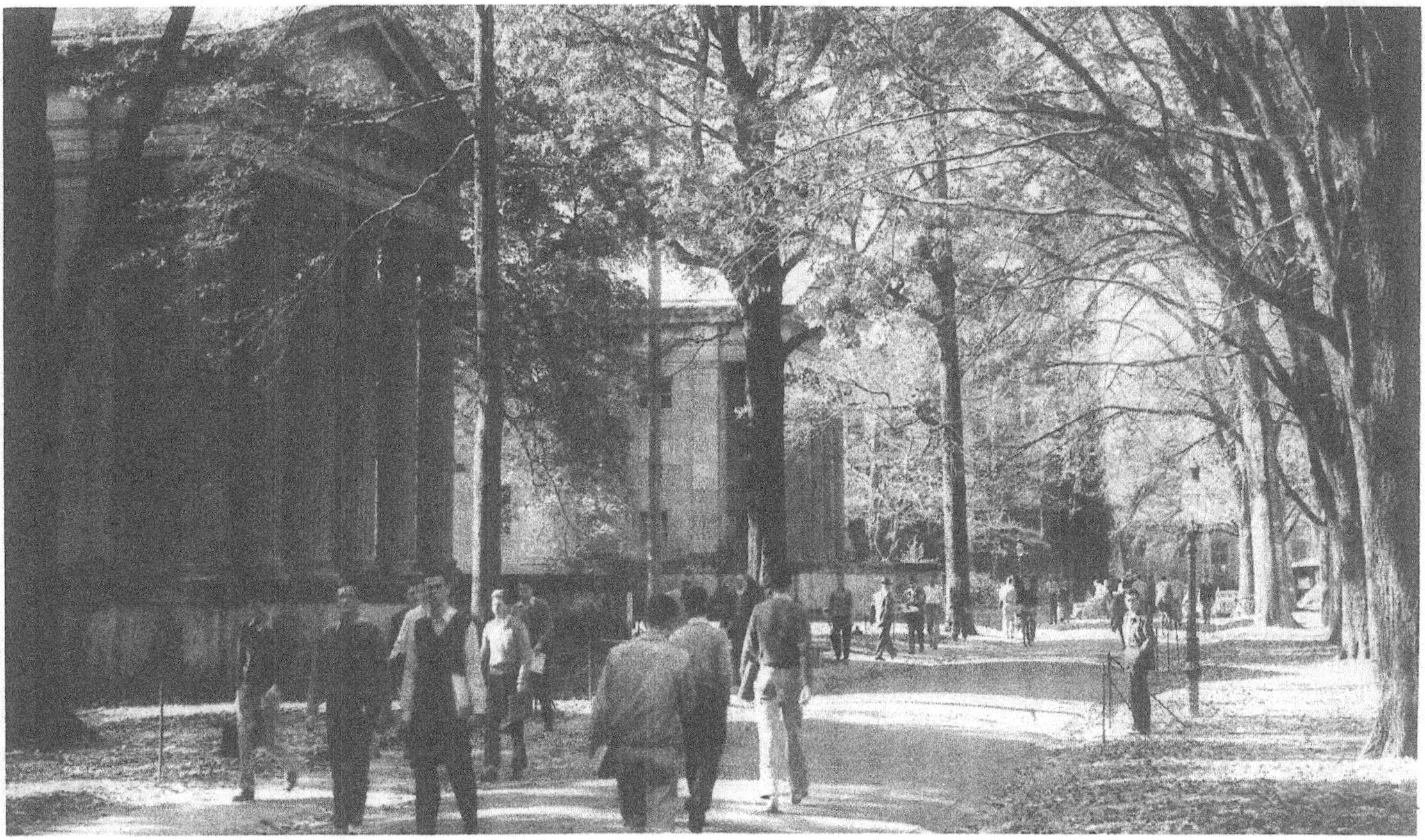

CLIO AND WHIG. Today these two organizations have combined to promote debating, public speaking, and interest in politics.

PRINCETON SUMMER CAMP, 1941. Since 1909 the Camp has been run by the Philadelphian Society or its present-day successor, the Student Christian Association. The Camp is now located at Blairstown. Some six thousand boys have received wholesome training and recreation, and six hundred Princeton undergraduates have served on the Camp's staff.

A Tub Race. The local lake provides all kinds of aquatic sports. In this event, in 1934, everyone got wet.

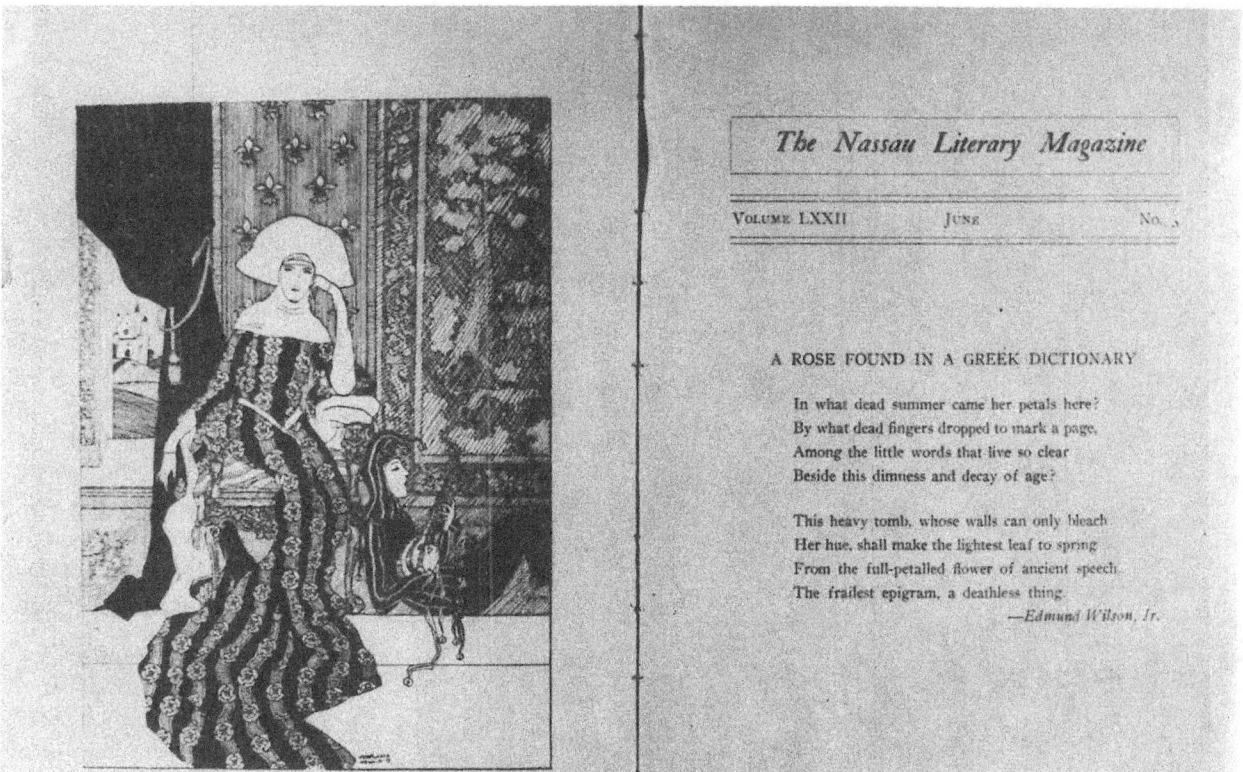

THE *Nassau Literary Magazine*. Founded in 1842, the *Nassau Lit,* as it is invariably called, is the oldest college literary periodical in America. Most Princeton alumni who have distinguished themselves in the world of letters either edited or wrote for the *Nassau Lit* in their undergraduate days. The magazine is now affiliated with The American Whig-Cliosophic Society.

Here are two pages from the issue of June 1916, including a poem by Edmund Wilson 1916.

Inauguration of "Johnny Maclean." The *Nassau Lit* is flourishing today, after a long and distinguished history. Other publications of the mid-nineteenth century had their brief moment of success and then disappeared. Among these were the *Cameleon* and *The Tattler* which appeared in the 1830's, *A Gem From Nassau's Casket* and *The Rattler* of the 1840's, and the *Nassau Rake* of the 1850's. The last had a flair for satire and cartoons. Its special issue for June 1854 satirized the inauguration of John Maclean as President.

COURTESY OF JOHN J. JOHNS 1920

Prince Board in 1879. Founded in 1876 and a daily since 1892 the *Princetonian* has long been known as the "most respected organization on the Campus." This undoubtedly is the most distinguished *Prince* board in its entire history. Seated, left to right: Robert H. McCarter 1879; Elwood O. Roessle 1879; Woodrow Wilson 1879; and Henry B. Fine 1880. Standing: Matthew G. Emery 1879; Charles A. Talcott 1879; William F. Magie 1879; Thomas D. Warren 1881; and George S. Johns 1880.

Reporting for the *Prince*. "Going out" for the *Prince* has always been a favorite activity for freshmen and sophomores who have a flair for journalism. Meeting a deadline can be fun, even if a candidate has to use one of the antiquated typewriters that never seem to get repaired.

The *Princeton Tiger* has supplied an outlet for undergraduate humor and sentiment since 1882. Interrupted by war, it has always been quickly revived.

This drawing by Booth Tarkington 1893 appeared in the issue of December 15, 1892. The caption reads:

Eminent Shade, "Aaron, a great many changes have come since our day. It doesn't look like the same place."

Contemporary, "Yes, there have been some changes, but there is the same old poller and there is the same old sport. Their clothes have changed, but they are the same, going in opposite directions and neither knowing what a good fellow the other is."

Newest of the general publications is *The Nassau Sovereign*, which first appeared shortly before World War II. Although its cartoons and drawings of glamour girls seem to have infringed upon territory claimed by the *Tiger*, its general articles and especially its polls of undergraduate opinion have won a wide audience. Its polls and "scientific" surveys cover every topic of student interest.

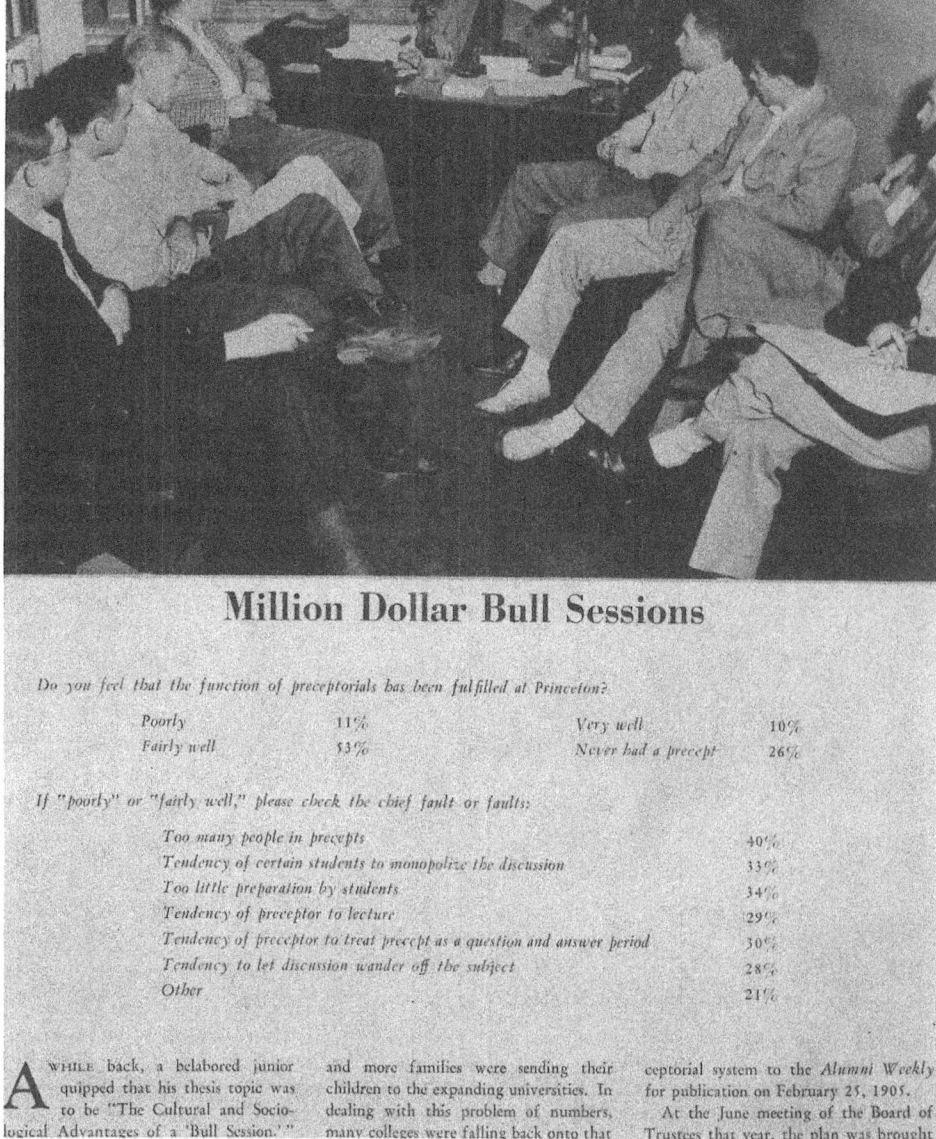

Million Dollar Bull Sessions

Do you feel that the function of preceptorials has been fulfilled at Princeton?

Poorly	11%	Very well	10%
Fairly well	53%	Never had a precept	26%

If "poorly" or "fairly well," please check the chief fault or faults:

Too many people in precepts	40%
Tendency of certain students to monopolize the discussion	33%
Too little preparation by students	34%
Tendency of preceptor to lecture	29%
Tendency of preceptor to treat precept as a question and answer period	30%
Tendency to let discussion wander off the subject	28%
Other	21%

A WHILE back, a belabored junior quipped that his thesis topic was to be "The Cultural and Sociological Advantages of a 'Bull Session.'" and more families were sending their children to the expanding universities. In dealing with this problem of numbers, many colleges were falling back onto that ceptorial system to the *Alumni Weekly* for publication on February 25, 1905.

At the June meeting of the Board of Trustees that year, the plan was brought

COLLEGE ORCHESTRA, 1868. Apparently the photographer always insisted upon an outdoors setting, but the heroic pose of the violinist seems hardly necessary. This is the first picture of an organization whose origin is lost in history.

GLEE CLUB on Tour, in 1886. A nonchalant pose is struck by the Glee Club which made an extensive tour in 1886. One member was apparently up all night. What was the shovel for? The Glee Club is still a most popular organization.

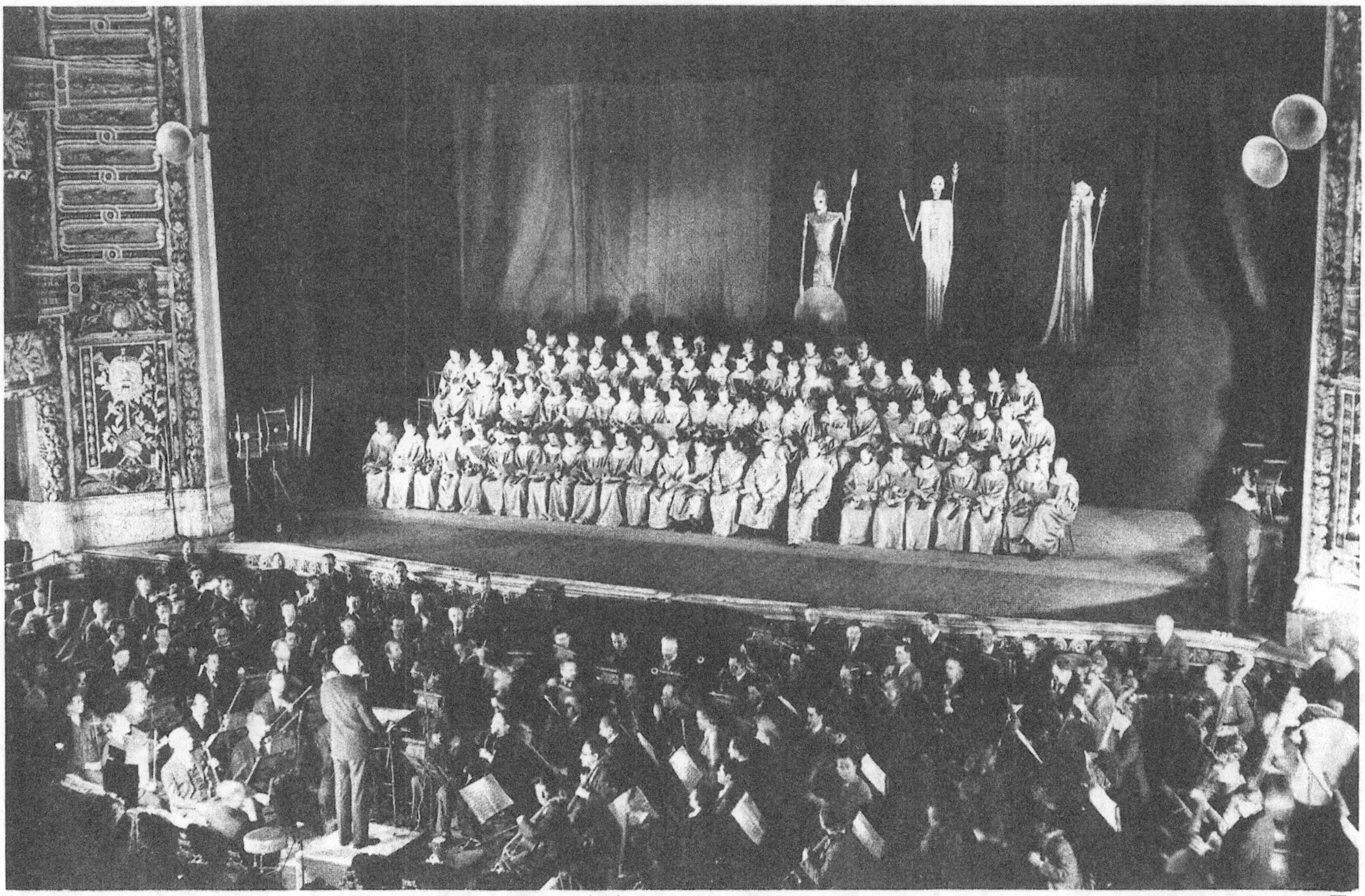

INTERNATIONAL NEWS PHOTO

Glee Club, Spring Tour, in 1931. A joint performance of *Oedipus Rex* with the Philadelphia Symphony Orchestra.

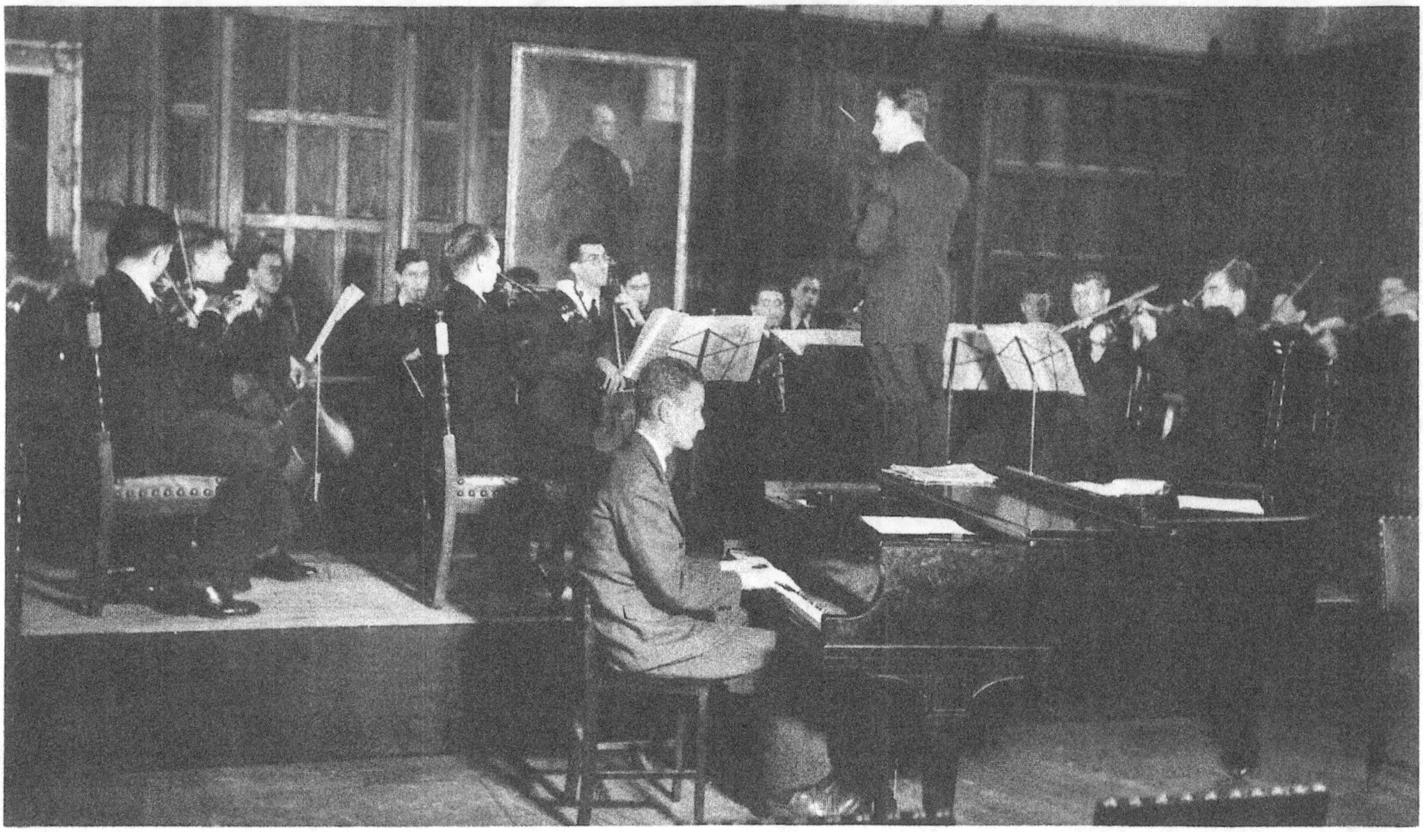

PHOTO BY MENZIES

Concert in Procter Hall. The University Orchestra gives numerous concerts. The pianist is Andrew W. Imbrie 1942.

PRINCETON BAND. This organization is most in evidence during the football season, but it also functions at parades and rallies.

Julius Caesar. Famous for fifty years, the TRIANGLE CLUB'S annual show brings forth the undergraduates' best efforts in song, dance, and acting. This is the cast of *Julius Caesar*, one of the greatest of Triangle shows and also one of the first. Written by Post Wheeler 1891 and Booth Tarkington 1893, it had an enormous success and was later revived. The role of Caesar was played by Shirrell N. McWilliams 1894 and that of Cassius by Tarkington. McWilliams is in the center with the laurel wreath; while Tarkington, with the lean and hungry look, is in armor on the right.

Triangle Love Scene. James Stewart 1932 is charmed by Harry H. Dunham 1933.

Feminine Despair. Dunham expresses frustration to Clinton E. Brush III 1933.

CLEAROSE STUDIO

Hamlet, by the THEATRE INTIME in 1927. William Brenton 1927 took the chief role, with Franklin Gary 1927 as Horatio and Charles E. Arnt, Jr., 1929 as Polonius. The Intime's productions have often received the applause of faculty critics.

151

OSLER'S EATING CLUB, 1862. During the 1840's both fraternities and eating clubs sprang up, but the former were banned in 1855. The early clubs appeared and dissolved yearly; most, like Old Bourbon and Hole in the Wall, were short-lived.

IVY CLUB, 1882. Oldest of the surviving clubs is Ivy which in 1882 was ensconced in Ivy Hall, the former Law School.

Social Life

PROSPECT AVENUE IN THE 1890's
Ivy and Tiger Inn are on the left, Cottage Club on the right.

The modern clubs, here and below, appear with their dates.

CAMPUS CLUB 1900

CANNON CLUB 1896

CAP AND GOWN CLUB 1894

CHARTER CLUB 1901

CLOISTER INN 1912

COLONIAL CLUB 1891

COTTAGE CLUB 1887

COURT CLUB 1921

DIAL LODGE 1908

ELM CLUB 1895

IVY CLUB 1879

KEY AND SEAL CLUB 1904

PROSPECT COOPERATIVE CLUB 1942

QUADRANGLE CLUB 1901

TERRACE CLUB 1904

TIGER INN 1890

TOWER CLUB 1902

The End Approaches

Senior Privilege. Only seniors may sit around the Mather Sun Dial, but the five minutes between classes does not give them much time to indulge in this privilege.

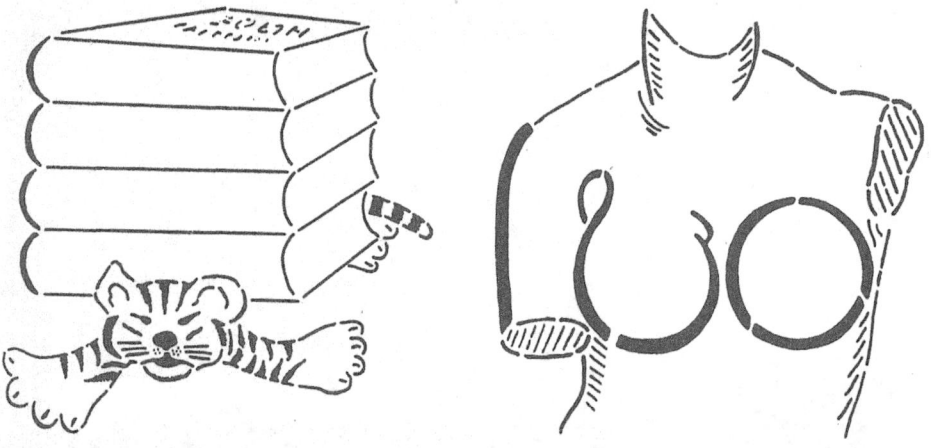

Beer Suit Designs. To save laundry bills, seniors adopted the practice of wearing "painter's suits" just before World War I. Soon each class adopted a distinctive design, and each spring now sees grave old seniors gaily disporting the new insigne on the back of their jackets. The design of the Class of 1925 expressed the pains incurred from the four-course plan, 1925 being the first class to be graduated under that dispensation. The Class of 1930 obviously thought itself the "perfect bust."

Houseparty Dance. Houseparty weekend is the climax of social activity in the spring term. Each generation of undergraduates has always claimed that the girls of that era are the prettiest; but 1946 does pretty well.

Cannon Exercises. Class Day exercises around the Cannon are noted for the long clay pipes which the seniors smoke and then break, and for the practical humor of the various "orations." Here Grant Sanger 1931, class secretary, is provided with office equipment for his new job.

Planting the Class Ivy. Nassau Hall is covered with ivy which has been planted by the various classes on Class Day, and stones are inserted to mark the individual vines. Here Walter M. Jenifer 1931 gets a young plant off to a good start.

Front Campus on Commencement Day. Weather permitting, the front campus is now the setting for graduation; otherwise the exercises are held in the Chapel. Here the Class of 1924 is earnestly studying the program.

Athletics

It is a truism that athletics have left a deep imprint upon Princeton and the alumni. Athletic sports began almost as soon as the founding of the College, but for a century they had little support from the faculty. The earliest games were hockey, handball, "a rustic brand of baseball, and a primitive form of football."

It was James McCosh who introduced a liberal attitude toward sports. His inaugural address called for physical training for all, and the building of the Bonner Gymnasium reflected an official approval of athletics. Since that time trustees and faculty alike have usually encouraged intercollegiate sports and have always strongly supported intramural athletics. Wilson was perhaps less enthusiastic toward the former than his predecessors, but under Hibben outstanding facilities, notably the Palmer Stadium and the Baker Rink, were constructed. Today practically every sport receives full and official recognition, with the important condition that the individual athlete must first and primarily be a student.

COURTESY OF W. M. BOYD

First Intercollegiate Football Game. PRINCETON AND RUTGERS played the first intercollegiate game of football on November 6, 1869, with the latter winning by 6 goals to 4. There were twenty-five men on each side. No photographer recorded this epoch-making event for history. (From the painting by William M. Boyd, Rutgers 1932.)

PRINCETON-YALE GAME, 1879. The year 1879 was the last in which Princeton played fifteen men on a team. This scene shows the St. George's Cricket Grounds at Hoboken. The score was 0 to 0, but the championship went to Princeton.

PRINCETON VS. COLUMBIA, 1889. The early years of intercollegiate football saw Yale and Princeton, and usually Harvard, dominant in the sport; other teams often took a merciless beating. Princeton defeated Columbia 71 to 0 in 1889, and the *Police Gazette* thought it a particularly rough game. Its artist depicted slugging, biting, heeling, strangling, gouging, kicking, and even the French sport of La Savate.

Gallantry before the Battle. Like most papers in the 1890's, the *Inquirer* delighted in depicting the pageantry of football games. But the smooth Pennsylvania captain is apparently making no progress with the current beauty, as long as the Princeton captain maintains his stern demeanor. The scene is the Germantown Cricket Club at Manheim. Pennsylvania first defeated Princeton in 1892.

PRINCETON VS. YALE, 1893. This game at Manhattan Field, which Princeton won by 6 to 0, was regarded as the greatest game of football ever played up to that time. Nearly fifty thousand saw the spectacle. Here Philip King 1893 places the ball in position for the initial rush of Princeton's flying wedge. (From *Leslie's Weekly*, December 7, 1893.)

"THE RIVALS" PENN AND PRINCETON IN THE GAY NINETIES

PHILADELPHIA INQUIRER

PRINCETON FOOTBALL. The "primitive form of football" dates from 1840, when opposing teams kicked a leather-covered bladder between East and West Colleges, a goal being scored when the ball hit either dormitory. The round rubber ball was first used in 1858.

With the beginning of intercollegiate contests, the rules of the game were slowly but necessarily clarified. The number of men on a team was reduced from twenty-five to fifteen and then, in 1880, to eleven. The soccer-like characteristics were lost as "downs" were substituted for the English "scrum" and the oval ball replaced the round. But it was not until 1906, when the forward pass was introduced, that the modern game finally emerged.

Princeton has long been proud of its tradition of alertness on the gridiron, and of its games won in the last few minutes of play. Old graduates still talk of such ancient feats as Jerry Haxall's sixty-five yard kick against Yale in 1882, Moffat's four goals against Harvard in 1883, Tilly Lamar's run at the close of the Yale game in 1885, Arthur Poe's hundred yard run that resulted in the only scoring in the Yale game in 1898, and John DeWitt's kick that beat Yale in 1903. Recent grads still enthuse over those hard-fought duels with Harvard after World War I, recall with sentiment those teams of Bill Roper's which couldn't be beaten because they wouldn't be beaten, and vividly remember the juggernauts of Crisler's day which smothered all opposition.

Princeton's overall record, at the close of 1946, comprises 448 victories, 41 ties, and 117 defeats. Its first match with Yale, in 1873, inaugurated a rivalry which is the oldest continuous series in football.

THE FAMOUS POE BROTHERS. For twenty years members of the Poe family of Baltimore made Princeton football famous. They won many games by their spectacular running and kicking. From left to right: Arthur Poe 1900; S. Johnson Poe 1884; Neilson Poe 1897 (in front); Edgar A. Poe 1891; Gresham H. Poe 1902; and John P. Poe 1895. Taken in 1902.

PRINCETON VS. HARVARD, 1911. This probably is the first aerial view of a football game, the picture being taken from a Wright biplane. The game was played on University Field, and Sanford B. (Sam) White's famous run brought Princeton the victory by 8 to 6. The same year White also beat Yale by another long run.

PRINCETON VS. CHICAGO, 1922. One of the greatest games in modern football was that between Princeton and Chicago in 1922, in which the "Team of Destiny" came from way behind to win by 21 to 18. Princeton's plunging halfback, Harry B. Crum 1924, here carries the ball; he never lost a yard in the entire game. The other Princeton man on his feet, in the left background, is Harland F. (Pink) Baker 1922, one of the Tiger's redoubtable tackles.

PRINCETON VS. HARVARD, 1926. The championship team of 1926 beat Harvard, 12 to 0, using every method of scoring. Here quarterback Dan P. Caulkins 1926 scores a touchdown on a double reverse from Slagle and Miles. Jacob W. (Jake) Slagle 1927 was one of the most versatile backs in Princeton's history. In 1925 his 82-yard run through the Yale team was the highlight of a championship season.

INTERNATIONAL NEWS PHOTO

INTERNATIONAL NEWS PHOTO

Bill Roper's Last Year. WILLIAM W. (Bill) ROPER 1902, Princeton's famous coach for two decades, is here in a familiar pose. He retired from coaching at the end of the 1930 season. In the center is Captain Ricardo A. Mestres 1931, and on the right is Albert Wittmer 1922, line coach who succeeded Roper as head coach.

An Allerdice Pass. DAVID W. ALLERDICE 1941 was the greatest passer in the history of Princeton football, and many were the games won by his accurate heaves, both long and short. Yale never had a chance when he was in college; and he is here shown throwing one to right end Howard J. Stanley 1941 (no. 42) for a gain of sixteen yards. This is the Yale game of 1938, won by 20 to 7.

PRESS ASSOCIATION, INC.

ACME PHOTO

Two Consistent Winners. The middle 1930's was the era of HERBERT O. (Fritz) CRISLER and some of the most powerful and versatile teams in Princeton's history. Here Crisler (left) watches practice with Pepper Constable 1936, captain and fullback of the championship team of 1935.

TAD WEIMAN and Robert L. Peters, Jr., 1942. Tad Weiman succeeded Crisler as football coach and had the distinction of beating Yale four times in a row, a feat Princeton had never accomplished before. Peters played three of those years, and as a senior was captain. In his last Yale game, when Princeton was trailing at the half way point, Peters entered the game despite a shoulder injury and scored three touchdowns. He was equally versatile in other sports. In the commencement baseball game with Yale in 1942, he drove two hits into the far stands and brought in seven runs.

Upset of the Year, 1946. PRINCETON beat PENNSYLVANIA by 17 to 14, in a major upset. In this scoring play a Penn kick has been blocked by Thomas G. Cleveland 1949, grandson of the late President. The ball was caught by Edward M. Mead 1949 who raced for one of the two Princeton touchdowns. In the last minute of play a field goal won the game.

PRINCETON'S FIRST NINE, 1860. Baseball proper began in Princeton in 1858, but the first outside game was played two years later. The Nassau nine ventured to Orange and the game was called on account of darkness when the score was 42 to 42! From left to right: H. H. Robinson 1862; Charles Young 1861; Henry Young 1862; Nehemiah Perry, Jr., 1861; E. H. Camp 1861; Captain L. W. Mudge 1862; J. L. Munn 1862; H. L. Sampson 1862; and L. H. Anderson 1861.

PRINCETON'S FIRST ATHLETIC FIELD. Baseball, cricket, and football were early played in the field southwest of Clio. The high wooden structure, on the left, was used as a wall in handball. This picture was taken about 1868.

UNIVERSITY FIELD, in the 1890's. Princeton athletes first used the field southwest of Clio, and then the "Princeton Grounds" at the foot of Chambers Street. In 1876 what is now University Field was purchased by the University Hotel Company, and subsequently title passed to the College. This view shows the wooden stands, Field House, and Cage.

A Trio of Princeton Athletic Figures, in 1915. Left to right: JOHN H. (Speedy) RUSH 1898; GEORGE R. (Joe) MURRAY 1893; and WILLIAM J. (Bill) CLARK. Rush was football coach during the seasons of 1915 and 1916. Murray was Graduate Manager of Athletics and Treasurer between 1900 and 1932. Clark came to Princeton as baseball coach in 1897 and retired in 1944.

HARRY C. DORER

Two Captains, a Few Years Apart. Two baseball captains meet before the commencement game with Yale in 1930. THE REVEREND EDWARD P. RANKIN 1865, captain of the team which played Princeton's first intercollegiate baseball game, with Williams in 1864; and JOHN H. O'TOOLE 1930. The Williams game was won by the score of 27 to 16; the Yale game by 6 to 4.

Spring Baseball Practice. Coach CHARLES W. CALDWELL 1925 looks over the hopeful efforts of candidates in the spring of 1946. Caldwell, who was one of Princeton's greatest pitchers and an outstanding halfback, came to Princeton after the war as coach of both baseball and football. In 1947 he relinquished the former position to concentrate on the latter.

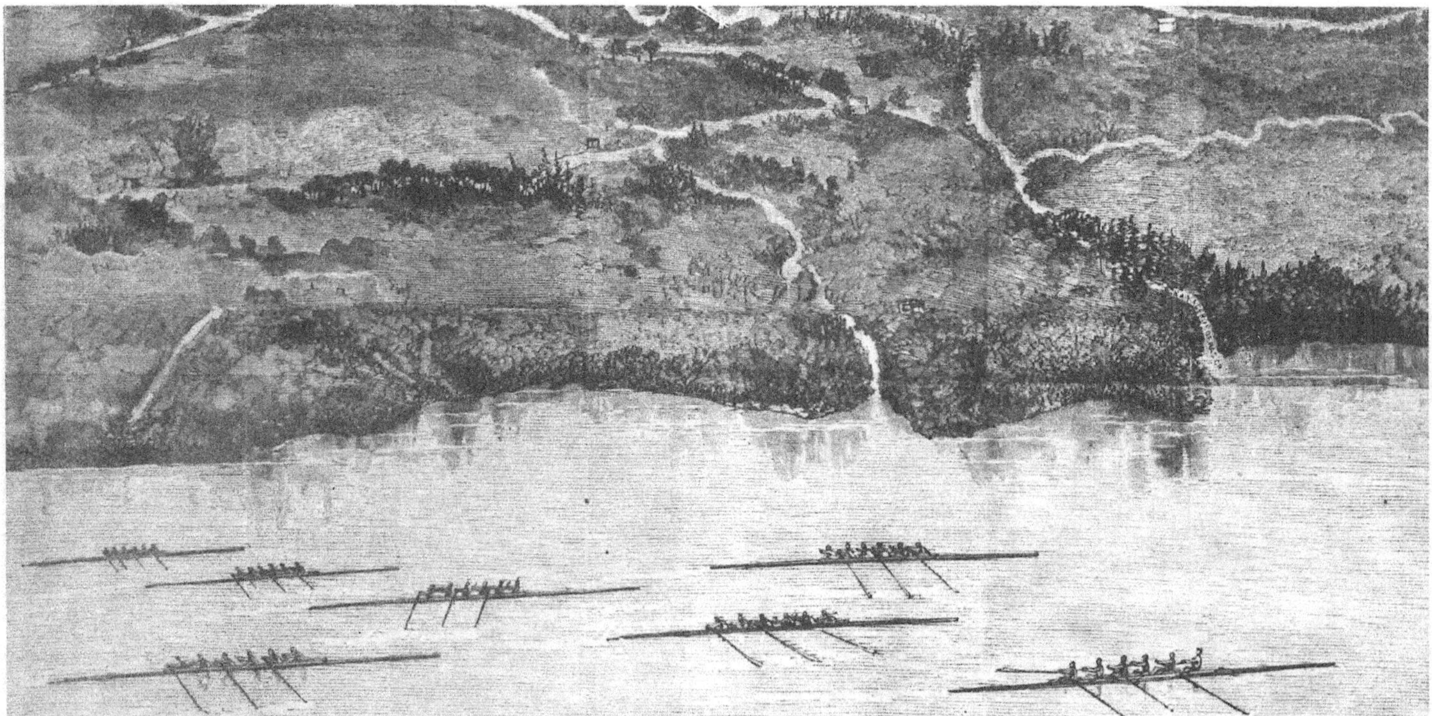

INTERCOLLEGIATE REGATTA AT SARATOGA, 1874. Princeton did not undertake rowing as an organized sport until 1870. Four years later freshman and varsity crews were sent to Saratoga and much to everyone's surprise the freshmen won over Brown and Yale. It was in this race that the colors of orange and black were first used. The varsity race was six-oared over a course of three miles; Columbia won and Princeton brought up the rear. (From *Harper's Weekly* of July 25, 1874.)

PHOTO BY BROWN BROTHERS

Carnegie Views His Loch. In 1884 rowing was abandoned as a sport as the difficulties of practicing on the narrow canal with its many barges were only too apparent. ANDREW CARNEGIE's gift of the lake in 1906 was hailed with joy by all hands. Mr. and Mrs. Carnegie visited Princeton in 1907 to see the first regatta. They followed the races from a boat on the canal. On the extreme left are Carnegie and Mrs. Moses T. Pyne.

Familiar Figure on the Lake. Professor J. DUNCAN SPAETH of the English Department, an old Pennsylvania oarsman, coached the Princeton crews for two decades. Some of Princeton's greatest crews were turned out under his tutelage in the years soon after World War I. On Spaeth's right is Alfred Noyes, distinguished English poet who was visiting professor at the time of this picture, in 1915.

CLASS OF 1887 BOAT HOUSE. This structure was erected in 1913, a few years after the creation of Lake Carnegie. It contains space for sixty-four shells. The Boat House, built near Washington Road, is comparatively near the campus; while the races are held on the lower section of the lake where the water is deeper.

INTERNATIONAL NEWS PHOTO

SPRING REGATTA, 1921. Princeton's great crew of 1921 defeating Navy, the Olympic champions, and Harvard, on Carnegie Lake. The shells have just crossed the finish line. The crew was stroked by John H. (Heinie) Leh 1921.

THE HENLEY ROYAL REGATTA, 1934. Leander beats Princeton by two-thirds of a length, winning the Grand Challenge Cup. Both crews broke the old course record. In an earlier race, the day before, Princeton had beaten Pembroke. This magnificent view of the Henley course was taken from the church tower near the finish line.

SPORT & GENERAL

GEORGE GOLDIE was Director of the Gymnasium and one of Princeton's prominent coaches between 1870 and 1911. Perhaps the greatest gymnast of his day, he popularized physical training. At the age of seventy-five, he performed a giant swing, and then handed in his resignation.

THE CALEDONIAN GAMES. These intra-mural track events, in which the four classes compete, have been a feature of Princeton athletics since 1873. They were started by George Goldie, and were so named because Goldie was then Caledonian champion.

The above picture is that of the finish of the half-mile in 1915; it shows Stuart K. Atha 1915 winning the event. Before the building of the Stadium, track events were held on University Field.

The picture below shows the high hurdle race in 1946. It was won by William M. Fitzpatrick 1949 (right). Victor A. Hansen 1949, David J. Seltzer 1948, and James B. Helme, Jr., 1946 (left) finished in that order.

Two Princeton Institutions, KEENE FITZPATRICK (left) and B. FRANKLIN BUNN 1907 are here shown before a track meet. From 1911 to 1933 Fitzpatrick was track coach and trainer at Princeton, thousands of undergraduates coming under the influence of his strong and sportsmanlike personality. He was generally recognized as the dean of college track coaches throughout the country.

B. Franklin Bunn, manager of the University Store, financial adviser to countless student organizations, and former Mayor of Princeton, has never been known to miss a track meet. He frequently acts as official.

Grand Slam in the 220-Yard Dash. Princeton and Harvard resumed track relations in 1932, after a lapse of six years; sports events between the two institutions had been broken off following the football season of 1926. At the meet in Palmer Stadium, in 1932, Princeton won by 75½ to 59½. Below, Hasket Derby 1932 (right) sets a new meet record at 21.6. Second place was won by Arthur D. Keown 1932 (center), and third by Ben H. Hand 1932.

Setting A World's Record, 1934. Princeton's greatest miler was WILLIAM R. BONTHRON 1934. At the Princeton Invitation Meet in 1933, both he and Jack Lovelock of New Zealand broke the world's record, Lovelock winning in 4:07.6. There followed a series of races between Bonthron and Lovelock and/or Glenn Cunningham of Kansas.

At the A.A.U. Championships in Milwaukee in June 1934, Bonthron set a new mark in the 1500-meter run, his time being 3:48.8. Bonthron is here shown beating Cunningham by only three-tenths of a second in that race, while Gene Venzke came in third.

INTERNATIONAL NEWS PHOTO

PRINCETON INVITATION MEET, 1935. The series of track meets held in Palmer Stadium in the 1930's brought outstanding runners from all over the world. Here Lovelock is winning the featured mile race in 4:11.2; while Bonthron is second, Cunningham third, and Venzke fourth. Because of its superior construction, the Stadium track is extremely fast.

AN EARLY CRICKET TEAM, 1864. Cricket was played as early as 1857 and prospered for some years despite the prediction of the *Nassau Lit* that the "college authorities would stop it, as there was something wicket in it." Princeton's first outside match was with Pennsylvania, in 1866. The sport was revived at the turn of the new century.

GYMNASIUM TEAM, 1872. The erection of the Bonner Gymnasium and the arrival of George Goldie as Director in 1870 resulted in a great enthusiasm for gymnastics. Local exhibitions became a regular feature of undergraduate life.

Hobart A. H. (Hobey) Baker 1914 was one of Princeton's greatest athletes. He captained both hockey and football teams, and was regarded as the leading amateur hockey player of his generation. Baker Rink stands as his memorial.

A Game for Tall Men. Captain Giles R. Scofield, Jr., 1939 taking one on the rebound in a basketball game with Yale on Alumni Day in 1939. The Tiger team won by 39 to 27.

R. V. C. WHITEHEAD, JR.

One Against Three. An unusual action shot in the Baker Rink. The hockey team of 1940-41 won the league championship, but in this game were tied by the St. Nicholas Club by 7 to 7, despite two overtime periods.

The Rink as Gymnasium. After the burning of the Gymnasium in 1944, the Baker Rink gave yeoman service. Here Ernest D. Pirman 1949 applies a squeeze on his Muhlenburg opponent.

ACTION ON THE OLD POLO FIELD, 1926. Since World War I, polo has been a popular sport. This is West Point vs. Princeton.

LACROSSE, on Franklin Field, Philadelphia. Lacrosse at Princeton dates back to 1881, and in recent decades the Tiger teams have competed successfully with Maryland's best. Here the championship team of 1929 beats Penn by 10 to 4.

RUGBY, introduced by English students after World War I, has steadily gained in favor, and several championship teams have been produced. This match with Cornell in 1939 resulted in a victory of 21 to 0.

THE MOST POPULAR SPORT. During the past three decades, tennis has usually been voted the most popular sport to play, and football that to watch. The first touch of spring always fills the courts, while even the faculty waits in line to sign up for the next day. Princeton teams have been consistent winners in the Eastern Intercollegiate League, and have sometimes met on even terms such redoubtable outfits as those from North Carolina and William and Mary.

THREE WORLD'S CHAMPION SWIMMERS. Princeton usually comes in second to Yale in the Eastern Intercollegiate Swimming League. The record for the 300-yard medley relay was broken several times in 1939. At the League championships at Yale that year, the Princeton trio set a new mark of 2:51.9. Princeton's medley relay team was composed of Albert Van de Weghe 1940 (left), Richard R. Hough 1939 (center), and Hendrick Van Oss 1939.

Not Too Hard. WILLIAM CAMPBELL 1945 sinks a putt on the Princeton course, watched by his teammate Jacques Houdry 1949 and Captain Rice of Dartmouth (center). Campbell, who served overseas in the artillery in World War II, won top honors in the Eastern Intercollegiates in 1946.

Alumni Reunions

No UNIVERSITY IN AMERICA has more loyal, affectionate, and generous alumni than Princeton. Historically, the alumni have played a major role in Princeton's development. When the College was at its nadir in the 1820's, it was the graduates who formed the Alumni Association of Nassau Hall and raised funds by which the faculty was strengthened and East and West Colleges built. In later years it was alumni influence, stimulated by President McCosh, which brought about a secularization of the College and lifted the dead hand of theological control. Eventually the alumni secured representation on the board of trustees, eight of them now being elected by ballot.

In 1909 the Graduate Council was formed, replacing an earlier Committee of Fifty which had secured funds to finance the preceptorial system. It was believed that there was other work to be done for the University, and today the Graduate Council regulates the affairs of the National Alumni Association and directs such activities as class affairs, regional alumni associations, schools and scholarships, public relations, undergraduate activities, placement, and the departmental advisory councils. The National Alumni Association, established in 1919, is a successor to the old Alumni Association of Nassau Hall.

Unlike such universities as Harvard, Yale, and Chicago, Princeton has had no benefactions of enormous size. Rather the endowment and buildings have largely been the result of many small and a few substantial gifts. For example, most of the campus dormitories have been named in honor of alumni who have generously contributed to Princeton's progress.

The affection with which graduates regard their alma mater is expressed not only in gifts but in frequent visits to the Princeton campus. Alumni reunions at commencement have long been famous; as many as 7,000 graduates have returned at one time. The custom goes far back in history, to the eighteenth century when commencement was held in the fall. In the late nineteenth century the practice began of wearing colored badges or hatbands to designate the reuning classes, and it remained for the twentieth to produce complete and colorful uniforms. The annual P-Rade, the singing of "Old Nassau," and the baseball game with Yale have long been a significant part of the Princeton tradition. As Dean Gauss has written, "Of course this is ritualism; it is the affirmation of the solidarity of the alumnus with his classmates and his college, the annual festival of initiation and rededication."

REUNION FOR 1879. The Class of 1879 at its twentieth reunion. This class, the most famous in modern Princeton history, produced one President, an Associate Justice of the Supreme Court, and a distinguished group of leaders in law, politics, business, education, and letters. Woodrow Wilson is in the upper left corner.

Ladies Reunion, 1902. Mrs. Hibben (right foreground) entertains the wives of 1882.

President Hibben Marches at Reunion.

Soldiers of the Revolution. The Class of 1903 parades at its tenth reunion.

The Statistics of 1877 are presented.

President Dodds, Edward D. Duffield 1892, and the Old Guard watch the P-Rade.

"Lamb" Heyniger 1916 leads "Old Nassau."

The Alumni P-Rade Meanders over University Field. The seniors bring up the rear; few parasols remain intact after the game.

The Highlanders Arrive, in 1946, carrying the 1934 banner.

A Class Baby of 1935 Marches with Grim Determination.

Nassau Street Scene. JAMES THAYER GEROULD, Librarian Emeritus, passes a foursome posing for a quick picture.

Reminiscing at Reunion. A group of 1905 men, including NORMAN THOMAS (right), relaxes and talks over old times.

Saturday Is Family Day, for 1925 at its twentieth.

The Corner of 1919's Tent, at Meal Time.

JOSEPH JANNEY STEINMETZ

Reunion for Two Deans. The Class of 1917 makes a double coup by inviting Dean Gauss (right) and Dean Heermance (in white) to its class dinner in 1937.

GRADUATE COUNCIL DINNER, 1946. At the head table, from left to right, are: Dean Godolphin, Lewis N. Lukens, Jr., 1917; Chauncey Belknap 1912; Richard K. Stevens 1922; President Dodds; Harold H. Helm 1920; Dean Gauss; Walter E. Hope 1901; John C. Williams II 1925; and R. Kenneth Fairman 1934.

PRESIDENT DODDS Addresses the National Alumni Association, at the 1946 Reunion. The front campus, on Sunday morning, is the setting for this event. The class standards indicate the number of alumni who served in the World Wars.

NATIONAL ALUMNI ASSOCIATION LUNCHEON, 1946. Because the Gymnasium had burned, the traditional alumni luncheon on Washington's Birthday was held in Baker Rink. Admiral King and Col. Franklin D'Olier 1898 gave the addresses

Princeton's Anniversaries

PRINCETON'S ANNIVERSARIES have been occasions not only for celebration but also for self-analysis. The centennial anniversary saw the College in a confident mood after its period of adversity; and unwisely, as it turned out, a Law School was inaugurated that was to fail only a decade later.

The sesquicentennial anniversary was chosen as the occasion for the change in name to university. By 1896 Princeton, with its achievements in scholarship and emphasis upon graduate work, was thoroughly deserving of its new name. To Andrew F. West is due much of the credit for the success of the celebration and especially the presence of distinguished delegates from foreign universities.

The bicentennial anniversary was celebrated during the academic year of 1946-1947. Appropriately the outstanding feature of the year's activities was the series of conferences in fifteen fields of learning, attended by over one thousand of the world's leading scholars and public figures. Most of these conferences, although based upon existing knowledge, were concerned with contemporaneous or future trends. As President Dodds pointed out, Princeton would not content herself with a merely self-congratulatory celebration; rather "our programs have all been oriented to the future, and discussions have not been devoted to reminiscences of past glories."

Invitation to the Centennial. Princeton's centennial anniversary would rightly have been celebrated on October 22, 1846; but because most of the Presbyterian synods were in session on that date, the ceremonies were postponed to June 1847.

JAMES CARNAHAN was President at the time of the centennial anniversary. It was under his administration that Princeton, having reached its low point in the 1820's, steadily grew in strength; by 1847 the College, with enlarged endowment and new buildings, faced the future with confidence. (From the portrait given to the University in the bicentennial year by G. Howard Bright 1894.)

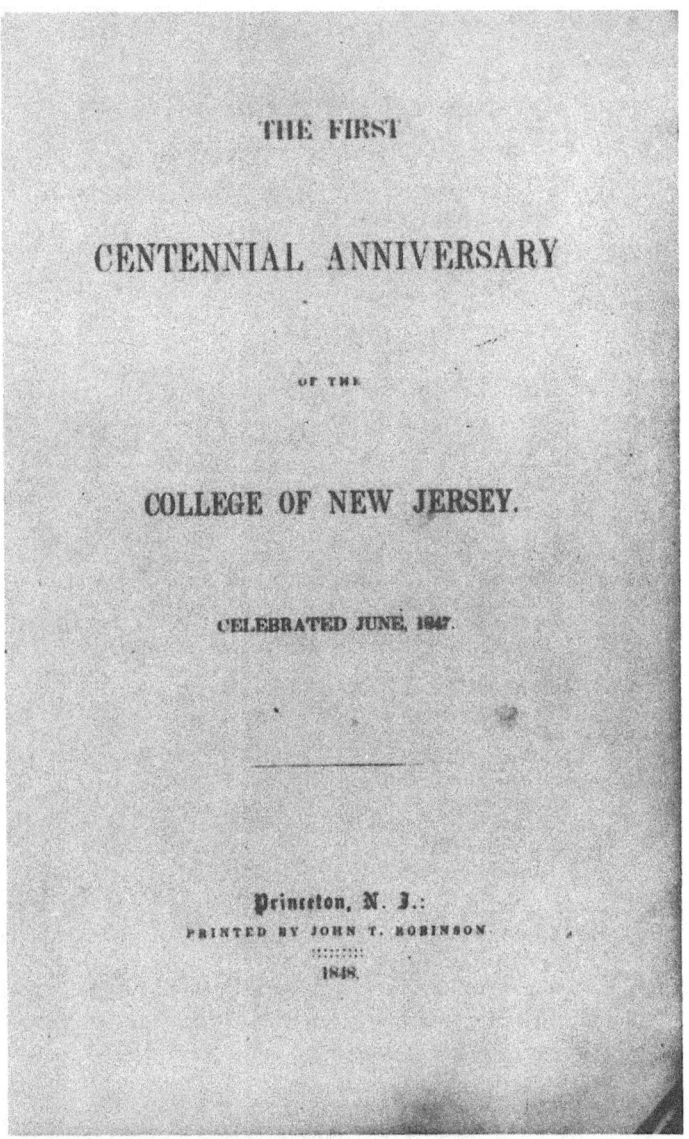

Account of the Centennial Anniversary. Title and first page of the booklet issued by the College; it relates the events during the two days of the celebration. Unfortunately few graphic memorabilia of the occasion have survived.

The Seal of Princeton University. The sesquicentennial anniversary of the College of New Jersey, in October 1896, was the occasion for the adoption of the new name of Princeton University. A new seal was designed by a committee of five trustees, of whom perhaps Moses T. Pyne 1877 was the most influential. The new seal was based in part upon the old one of the College of New Jersey. In the upper part or chief of the shield is an open Bible taken directly from the old. In the lower part is a chevron, denoting the rafters of a building. Between the sides of the shield and the circle is the ancient motto, *Dei sub numine viget*. Both the old and the new seals are to be found on the campus as, for example, on FitzRandolph Gateway.

The Sesquicentennial Celebration. Nassau Street (left) was decorated in all its glory for the occasion. The old Nassau Inn did itself especially proud with its flags and bunting.

Academic Procession. Alumni and townspeople were interested spectators of the procession as it wound through the campus to Alexander Hall.

Many delegates from foreign universities brought greetings to Princeton and several of them gave public lectures as part of the ceremonies. From left to right (left center) are Professor Felix Klein of the University of Göttingen; Professor Edward Dowden of the University of Dublin; and Professor Arnold A. W. Hubrecht of the University of Utrecht.

Memorial Arch. In honor of the sesquicentennial the borough of Princeton erected two arches on Nassau Street: one in front of the First Presbyterian Church, the other at the Princeton Bank and Trust Company.

ROSE AND SON

Princeton's sesquicentennial celebration lasted three days. On October 20, after the academic procession had entered Alexander Hall, President Patton delivered a sermon in which he pledged the adherence of the College to the religious ideals of the past. In the afternoon an address of welcome was followed by responses by President Eliot of Harvard and Professor J. J. Thomson of the University of Cambridge. In the evening a concert was given under the direction of Walter Damrosch.

On October 21, Henry van Dyke 1873 read his anniversary ode, *The Builders*, which was followed by Wilson's address. That evening a long torchlight parade, headed by the 71st Regimental Band of New York and Chief Marshal William Libbey 1877, was reviewed by President and Mrs. Grover Cleveland in front of Nassau Hall (lower left). In addition to Princeton alumni and undergradutes, the procession included a delegation of seniors from Yale. Nassau Hall was illuminated by hundreds of electric lights (lower right) while the campus was further made gay by Chinese lanterns and a display of fireworks.

On October 22, a final convocation was held at which Patton announced the change in name to Princeton University, a large number of honorary degrees were granted, and a concluding address was delivered by President Cleveland.

Professor Woodrow Wilson. Among the many public addresses during the celebration, the most notable was that by Woodrow Wilson, entitled *Princeton in the Nation's Service*. For fifty years it has been widely quoted. This is from a photograph of Wilson taken before the sesquicentennial.

A. W. RICHARDS

Opening of the Bicentennial Year. The academic procession on September 22, 1946, at the opening of Princeton's bicentennial year. President Dodds and the Most Reverend Geoffrey Francis Fisher, Archbishop of Canterbury, lead the procession from the Chapel to Nassau Hall. Governor Walter E. Edge follows. The Archbishop delivered the first in the series of Bicentennial Sermons, and later received the degree of Doctor of Divinity in the Faculty Room.

Charter Day. The celebration of Charter Day, in October 1946, saw a long academic procession cross the campus to the convocation in the Chapel. The top view shows a section of the faculty in front of West College.

Following the Charter Day convocation, those receiving honorary degrees gathered on the steps of Nassau Hall. Front row, left to right: Walter E. Hope 1901, University Orator; Niels Bohr, physicist; President Dodds; Professor Yuen Ren Chao, Tsing Hua University; Sir Henry Hallett Dale; and Chauncey Belknap 1912, Chief Marshal. Second row: President Frank P. Graham, University of North Carolina; Sir Harold Hartley; Sir Hector James Wright Hetherington; Professor Frank H. Knight; Trygve Lie; and Baron Lindsay of Birker, Master of Balliol College. Third row: Professor Cyril N. H. Long, Yale University; Salvador de Madariaga y Rojo, Spanish historian; Jacques Maritain, French Ambassador to the Vatican; Professor Charles H. McIlwain 1894, Harvard University; and Professor Charles E. Merriam, University of Chicago. Fourth row: Professor Reinhold Niebuhr, Union Theological Seminary; Professor Marjorie H. Nicolson, Columbia University; Sir John Boyd Orr, Director-General Food and Agriculture Organization, UN; Professor Linus C. Pauling, California Institute of Technology; Professor Michael Polanyi, University of Manchester; and Professor Cornelis B. Van Niel, Stanford University. Back row: President Henry M. Wriston, Brown University; and Professor Ernest L. Woodward, University of Oxford.

Several of the recipients of honorary degrees. From right to left are Trygve Lie, Secretary General of the United Nations; Professor Frank H. Knight, University of Chicago; Sir Hector James Wright Hetherington, Principal of the University of Glasgow; Sir Harold Hartley, Chairman, British Overseas Airways; and Sir Henry Hallett Dale, Director of Laboratories of Royal Institution.

Charter Day Procession. On leaving the Chapel, the Chief Marshal is followed by Governor Edge and President Dodds.

Conferences of Scholars. The distinguishing feature of Princeton's bicentennial year was the series of three-day conferences in fifteen fields of learning. The first sessions were held in the Graduate College with occasional public lectures given in McCarter Theater or on the campus.

The first subject was The Future of Nuclear Science. Here are five Nobel Prize Winners who attended; from left to right: Professor P. A. M. Dirac, University of Cambridge; M. G. Mescheryskov, Lenin Institute for Radium; Madame Irene Curie-Joliot, Laboratoire de Chemie of the College de France; Professor Niels Bohr, Universitetets Institut for Teoretisk Fysik; and Chancellor Arthur H. Compton, Washington University.

Informal Conference. Three of the world's leading scientists and administrators chat between sessions at the Graduate College. From left to right: Professor Eugene P. Wigner, Princeton University; President Karl T. Compton, Massachusetts Institute of Technology; and President James B. Conant, Harvard University.

Conference Interlude. Two delegates to the conference on the Chemistry and Physiology of Growth consult informally. Professor Cyril N. H. Long, now Dean of the Yale Medical School (left), and Dr. Oscar Schotte of Amherst College (right).

The First Princeton-Rutgers Game. The football game between Princeton and Rutgers on Charter Day, October 19, 1946, saw a realistic (?) reenactment of the first game played in 1869. Here a Princeton flying wedge hurls a would-be Rutgers tackler to the rear, while the referee looks askance at the play. The reenactment was carried out between the halves of the regular game, and was enlivened with ancient costumes, bicycles, and carryalls.

Dedication of Joseph Henry Murals. One of the more festive ceremonies held in connection with the conference on Engineering and Human Affairs was the dedication of the murals in the Engineering Building, in October 1946. Painted by Gifford R. Beal 1900, the murals depict the scientific experiments carried out by Joseph Henry, professor of natural philosophy 1832-1848. From left to right are: Kenneth H. Condit 1913, Dean of the School of Engineering; Mr. Beal; and President Harold W. Dodds.

Conference Dinner. Delegates to the first series of conferences were housed in the Graduate College. Meals were provided in Procter Hall. This is a dinner for those attending the conference on The Development of International Society. After the graduate students returned, the Princeton Inn was used as the center for visiting scholars.

Post-Conference Discussion. The close of the conference periods usually was followed by informal discussions going on far into the night, during which Princeton faculty members met the visiting delegates. From left to right: Professor Charles H. McIlwain 1894, Harvard University; Professor Edward M. Earle, Institute for Advanced Study; Professor Carl Remer, University of Michigan; and Professor William W. Lockwood, Dean J. Douglas Brown 1919, and Professor Frank A. Fetter, all of Princeton.

Three Presidents Compare Notes. The conference on The Evolution of Social Institutions in America saw a notable group of educators assembled in the Graduate College. Here are conferring, from left to right: President John E. Pomfret, The College of William and Mary; President Henry P. Van Dusen 1919, Union Theological Seminary; and President Howard F. Lowry, the College of Wooster. Both Pomfret and Lowry had been members of the Princeton faculty some years before.

ORREN JACK TURNER

A Group of Humanists. The sixth conference brought an outstanding group of humanists to the Graduate College. Discussion centered on The Humanistic Tradition in the Century Ahead. This group picture was made between sessions.

Front row, left to right: President Herbert Davis, Smith College; Professor David N. Smith, Oxford University; Professor Salvador de Madariaga y Rojo, Oxford University; Professor Margaret Gilman, Bryn Mawr College; Dr. Alexander D. Lindsay, Oxford University; Professor Marjorie H. Nicolson, Columbia University; Professor Donald A. Stauffer 1923, Princeton University; President James B. Conant, of Harvard University; Sir Hector J. W. Hetherington, University of Glasgow; Professor Lily R. Taylor, Bryn Mawr College; Professor Edmundo O'Gorman, University of Mexico; the Reverend Reinhold Niebuhr, Union Theological Seminary; and Dr. James R. Angell, past President of Yale University.

Second row: Mr. Ernest H. Wilkins, President of the Modern Language Association; Professor Michael Karpovich, Harvard University; Dean Boris Mirkine-Guetzevitch, Ecole Libre des Hautes Etudes; Professor Ralph B. Perry, Harvard University; Professor F. O. Matthiessen, Harvard University; Professor Ernest J. Simmons, Columbia University; Professor Robert R. Palmer, Princeton University; Professor Robert M. MacIver, Columbia University; Professor Arthur D. Lovejoy, the Johns Hopkins University; Dr. Walter W. Stewart, Institute for Advanced Study; Dr. Frank Aydelotte, Director of the Institute for Advanced Study; Dr. Artur Schnabel; Professor Leo Spitzer, the Johns Hopkins University; Professor Lyman Bryson, Columbia University; and Mr. Harold Spivacke, Library of Congress.

Third row: Dr. Francis H. Taylor, Director of the Metropolitan Museum of Art; Professor Wolfgang Stechow, Oberlin College; President Lynn T. White, Mills College; Mr. Archibald MacLeish; Professor Louis Gottschalk, University of Chicago; Professor Jacques Barzun, Columbia University; Dean Richard F. McKeon, University of Chicago; Dr. Theodor E. Mommsen, Princeton University; Professor I. A. Richards, Harvard University; Professor Charles W. Hendel 1913, Yale University; Dean James S. Wilson, University of Virginia; Professor Howard M. Jones, Harvard University; Professor Werner W. Jaeger, Harvard University; and Professor William A. Nitze, University of Chicago.

Top row: Professor Rensselaer W. Lee 1920, College Art Association of America; Professor Edward F. D'Arms 1925, University of Colorado; Mr. John Marshall, Rockefeller Foundation; Professor Glen Haydon, University of North Carolina; Professor Sturgis E. Leavitt, University of North Carolina; Professor Hajo Holborn, Yale University; Mr. W. H. Auden; Professor George H. Sabine, Cornell University; and Dean John W. Dodds, Stanford University.

Two world famous scientists, Edwin Grant Conklin (left) and Dr. J. B. S. Haldane (right) apparently approach the subject of their conversation from different points of view.

JAMES V. FORRESTAL 1915, Secretary of the Navy, directed the conference on University Training for Public Service. At its conclusion he addressed a large audience at McCarter Theater.

HISTORIAN ARNOLD J. TOYNBEE addresses a capacity audience in McCosh 50 on the rise and fall of past civilizations.

Principal speaker at the Alumni Day Luncheon on February 22 was SECRETARY OF STATE GEORGE C. MARSHALL, who had earlier received the degree of Doctor of Laws. His address stressed the need of a sense of responsibility for world order.

During the final ceremonies at the end of the bicentennial year, the cornerstone of the Harvey S. Firestone Memorial Library was laid. Here David H. McAlpin 1920 (right), chairman of the Trustees' Committee on the Library, lowers the cornerstone box. On the left is Harvey S. Firestone, Jr., 1920, whose family was the principal donor of the Library.

PHOTO BY MENZIES

PHOTO BY MENZIES

The academic procession on June 16, 1947, included over four hundred delegates from universities and learned societies. Leading the procession are marshals George A. Graham and E. Baldwin Smith, while immediately behind is Professor Jesús Cosin of the Universidad de Salamanca, the oldest university represented. Then follow the two delegates from the Université de Paris. The United States Marine Band played the processional music.

In Alexander Hall (below) President Dodds greets Sir James Irvine, Principal of St. Andrews, who spoke for the foreign delegates. Seated at the right is President Conant of Harvard, spokesman for the American delegates.

Bicentennial Dinner. The new Dillon Gymnasium was the setting for the banquet held for alumni and visiting delegates. Walter E. Hope 1901 presided, and the speakers included Dr. Douglas S. Freeman; Governor Alfred E. Driscoll; President Mildred McA. Horton of Wellesley; President Charles Seymour of Yale; Field Marshal Viscount Alexander of Tunis, the Governor-General of Canada; and former President Herbert C. Hoover. The last officially represented Stanford University, and he has here (left) just concluded his address as Viscount Alexander turns to applaud.

A. W. RICHARDS

Five White House Residents. Prospect was the scene of colorful activity on June 17 when the presidential party from Washington joined the guests already assembled. The five past or present residents of the White House are, from left to right: Mrs. Truman; Mrs. Thomas J. Preston (the former Mrs. Cleveland); President Harry S. Truman; Herbert C. Hoover; and Mrs. Woodrow Wilson.

A Group in the Garden at Prospect. From left to right: General Dwight D. Eisenhower; President Truman; Herbert Hoover; President Dodds; and Sir James Irvine. The first two received the degree of Doctor of Laws.

ROSE AND SON

PHOTO BY MENZIES

Academic Procession, June 17. The longest academic procession in Princeton's history passed from Holder Hall to the front campus where the final convocation of the bicentennial year was held. Here the foreign delegates are led through Campbell arch by marshals Albert Elsasser and Daniel C. Sayre. The delegates from Salamanca, Paris, Oxford, Cambridge, Toulouse, Karlova, and other universities follow in order of precedence set by the age of their respective institutions.

PHOTO BY MENZIES

PRESIDENT TRUMAN made the principal address at the final convocation on the front campus. He has here just received the degree of Doctor of Laws from President Dodds (right). Standing on the left are Frederick M. Vinson, Chief Justice of the United States, who received a similar degree; Herbert C. Hoover, who received the same degree in 1917; and Chauncey Belknap 1912, Chief Marshal of the procession. Altogether, thirty-seven honorary degrees were awarded.

Final Convocation of the Bicentennial Year. The front campus held an overflow audience of 6,500 at the concluding ceremony of the bicentennial year. President Dodds, the only speaker besides President Truman, opens the convocation.

PHOTO BY MENZIES

The obverse of the Bicentennial Medal of Princeton University.

Index

Account Book of Aaron Burr, 10
Account of the College, 12
Alexander, Stephen, 25, 26, 27
Alexander Hall, 78
Alumni reunions, 176-180
Alumni, distinguished, 14-18, 51-56
American Whig Society, see The Halls
Arcade Theater, 138
Archaeological expeditions, 67
Army Post Exchange School, 114
Athletics, undergraduate, 158-175
Atomic research, 116
Bachelors Club, 69
Baker, Hobart A. H., 173
Baker Memorial Skating Rink, 101
Band, Princeton, 150
Baseball, 68, 164-166
Basketball, 173
Battle of Princeton, 105, 106
Belcher, Jonathan, 6
Belknap, Chauncey, 74, 187, 196
Beer suit designs, 156
Bicentennial Celebration, 185-197
Bicentennial Conferences, 188, 190-193
Bicentennial Medal, 197
Biddle, Nicholas, 56
Blair, Francis P., Jr., 53
Blair Hall, 80
Boker, George H., 55
Bonthron, William R., 171
Boudinot, Elias, 13
Brackett, Cyrus F., 27, 28
Brakeley, George A., 74
British Indoctrination, 115
Brown, J. Douglas, 61, 75, 190
Brown, Joseph, 124
Brown Hall, 77
Bunn, B. Franklin, 73, 170
Burr, Aaron, 2, 10
Burr, Aaron, (Jr.), 16
Butler, Howard C., 67
Caldwell, Charles W., 166
Campbell Hall, 84
Campus views: Dawkins engraving, 10; Bufford lithograph, 31; west campus, 37, 38, 79; Robertson, Seibert and Shearman lithograph, 34; Hudnut lithograph, 47; east campus, 49; front campus life, 49; aerial views, 100-102
Campus Club, 153
Cane spree, 132
Cannon, 43
Cannon Club, 153
Cap and Gown Club, 153
Carnahan, James, 21, 181
Carnegie, Andrew, 70, 167
Carpenter, William S., 75
Centennial Celebration, 181, 182
Chapel: Old, 32, 43; Marquand, 48, 49; New, 95, 96

Charter of College, 5
Charter Club, 153
Chemical Laboratory: Old, 77; Henry C. Frick, 97
Christian Student, 81
Civil War, 107
Clark, William J., 165
Class of 1877 Laboratory, 50, 104
Class of 1879, 136, 176
Class of 1879 Hall, 82
Class of 1887 Boat House, 167
Class of 1901 Hall, 90, 91
Class of 1903 Hall, 93
Class of 1904—Henry Hall, 90, 115
Class of 1905—Foulke Hall, 90
Class Day, 157
Class Rush, 133, 134
Cleveland, Grover, 184
Cliosophic Society, see The Halls
Cloaca Maxima, 41
Cloister Inn, 153
Clothes, undergraduate, 135
Colonial Club, 154
Commencement: account of 1748, 7-8; theses of 1750, 9; 1878, 27; honorary degrees, 72, 76; wartime, 113, 114; modern, 157
Company L, 109
Condit, Kenneth H., 65, 113, 189
Cottage Club, 154
Courses, 118, 120, 122, 123, 124, 125, 127
Court Club, 154
Crew, 166-168
Crisler, Herbert O., 163
Customs and traditions, undergraduate, 128-142
Cuyler Hall, 86
Dallas, George M., 53
Davies, Samuel, 3
Dean's House, 10, 39
Dial Lodge, 154
Dickinson, Jonathan, 2
Dickinson Hall, 41
Diploma, 12
Dodds, Harold W., 59, 74, 76, 113, 177, 179, 180, 185, 187, 189, 194, 195, 196, 197
Dodds, Mrs. Harold W., 115
Duffield, Edward D., 177
East College, 29, 31, 34
Edison, Thomas A., 72
Edwards, Jonathan, 3
Edwards Hall, 40
Eisenhart, Luther P., 61, 73
Elliott, Edward G., 63
Ellsworth, Oliver, 15
Elm Club, 154
Employment, student, 142
Engineering Building, J. C. Green, 97
English Department, 70
Eno Hall, 94

Ewing, John, 17
Examinations, 119-121
Faculty, 23-28, 60-76, 116, 117, 118, 120, 122, 124, 167
Faculty Room, 82
Farrand, Livingston, 54
Fine, Henry B., 60, 146
Fine Hall, 98
Finley, Samuel, 4
Finney, John M. T., 55
Firestone, Harvey S., Jr., 113, 193
Fitzpatrick, Keene, 170
Flour picture, 131
Football, 158-163, 189
Fox, Col. Arthur E., 113
Frelinghuysen, Theodore, 52
Freneau, Philip, 18
Friend, Albert M., Jr., 89
Gauss, Christian, 64, 73, 179
George II, King, 6
General Account, 8
Geology expeditions, 66
Geology Summer School, 127
Glee Club, 148, 149
Godolphin, Francis R. B., 64, 179
Goethals, Gen. George W., 72
Goldie, George, 27, 169
Graduate College, 87, 88, 114
Graduate Council, 179
Green, Ashbel, 20
Greene, Arthur M., Jr., 64, 73
Gymnasium: First, 34; Bonner, 35, 37; Recent, 81; Dillon, 103
Guyot, Arnold H., 25, 26, 27, 39
Guyot Hall, 84
Hall, Walter P., 120
Halls, The, 31, 78, 143
Hamilton Hall, 86
Hazing, 130
Heermance, Radcliffe, 65, 73, 179
Henry, Joseph, 23, 24, 189
Henry House, 30, 31, 34
Hepburn, James C., 54
Heyniger, C. Lambert, 177
Hibben, John G., 59, 71, 72, 73, 177
Hockey, 173
Hodge, Charles, 53
Holder Hall, 85
Honor System, 121
Hoover, Herbert C., 72, 194, 195, 196
Horsing, 131
Houseparty dance, 156
Housing, congressional, 13
Industrial Relations Section, 75
Isabella McCosh Infirmary: Old, 77; New, 94
Ivy Club, 152, 154
Ivy Hall, 33, 152
Jerome, Leonard W., 56
Johnson, Jimmy, 30, 142
Junior Hi-Hat Parade, 139
Key and Seal Club, 155

199

Kirkland, Samuel, 17
Kissam, Philip, 118
Ladenburg, Rudolf W., 117
Langfeld, Herbert S., 122
Laughlin Hall, 91
Law School, see Ivy Hall
Lee, Henry, 17
Libbey, William, 72
Library: Catalogue, 12; in Nassau Hall, 36; Chancellor Green, 42, 43; Pyne, 79; Firestone, 104, 193
Lindsley, Philip, 22
Little, Stafford, Hall, 80
Livingston, Edward, 16
Lockhart Hall, 92
Log College, 5
Lottery, 11
McAlpin, David H., 193
McCarter Theater, 91
McClenahan, Howard, 63
McCormick Hall, 93
McCosh, James, 22, 26, 27, 45, 46
McCosh Hall, 83
McCosh Walk, 46
McIlvaine, Charles P., 54
McMaster, John B., 28
Maclean, John, (Sr.), 25
Maclean, John, 21, 24, 26, 145
Madison, James, 12, 14
Madison Hall, 89
Magie, William F., 60, 66, 73, 146
Mann, Thomas, 76
Manning, James, 17
Marquand, Allan, 28
Marquand Chapel, 48, 49
Marshall, Gen. George C., 193
Martin, Luther, 15
Materials Testing Laboratory, 118
Mather Sun Dial, 68, 83, 156
Morey, Charles R., 67
Murray, George R., 165
Murray, James O., 27
Murray Dodge Hall, 81
Museum of Historic Art, 50
Nassau Club, 99
Nassau Hall, viii, 10, 11, 31, 34, 36, 47, 49, 82
Nassau Literary Magazine, 145
Nassau Rake, 145
Nassau Sovereign, 147
Nassau Street, 47
National Alumni Association, 180
Naval Training Units, 110, 114
Observatory: Old, 37; of Instruction, 50; New, 98
Ogden, Aaron, 16

Orchestra, 148, 149
Osborn, Henry F., 54
Osler's Club, 152
Palmer Physical Laboratory, 83
Palmer Stadium, 102
Paterson, William, 15
Patton, Francis L., 58
Patton Hall, 82
Philosophical Hall, 31, 34
Poe Brothers, 160
Poler's recess, 138
Preceptorial of the Air, 116
Preceptorial System, 122
President's House, see Dean's House
Presidents, portraits of, 2-4, 20-22, 58-59, 72, 76, 182
Princeton, U.S.S., 118
Princeton Flying School, 108
Princeton Packet, 13
Princeton Surveys, 75
Princeton Tiger, 147
Princeton University Press, 99
Princetonian, 146
Proclamation, sophomore, 130
Proctors, 98, 140, 141
Prospect, 45
Prospect Avenue, 153
Prospect Cooperative Club, 155
Publications, undergraduate, 145-147
Pyne, Moses T., 56, 70, 71
Pyne Hall, 89, 90
Quadrangle Club, 155
Raycroft, Joseph E., 73
Reed, Joseph, 16
Refectory, 33
Reserve Officers' Training Corps, 111
Reunion Hall, 38
Revolutionary War, 105, 106
Riots, 137
Rooms, undergraduates, 128-129
Roosevelt, Jacobus (James), 18
Root, Robert K., 61
Roper, William W., 162
Rush, Benjamin, 18
Rush, John H., 165
Rush, Richard, 52
Saint Patrick's Day Parade, 139
School of Public and International Affairs, 126
School of Science Building, J. C. Green, 44
Scott, William B., 66
Scribner, Charles, 56
Seal: of College, 8; of University, 182
Sesquicentennial Celebration, 182-184
Shippen, William, 18
Sly, John F., 75

Smith, Samuel S., 20
Smyth, Henry D., 116
Snow fight, 132, 134
Spaeth, J. Duncan, 167
Spanish American War, 108
Sports, minor, 172-175
Stanhope Hall, 29, 31, 34
Stealing clapper, 132
Stillwell, Richard, 67
Stockton, Richard, 15
Stockton, Commodore Robert F., 53
Student Christian Association, 144
Students' Army Training Corps, 109, 110
Summer Camp, 144
Swimming pool, 103
Taft, William H., 71
Tarkington, Booth, 55, 147, 150
Taylor, Hugh S., 63, 116
Tennent, Gilbert, 6
Terrace Club, 155
Theatre Intime, 151
Tiger Inn, 155
Torrey, John, 25
Tower Club, 155
Track, 169-171
Triangle Club, 150, 151
Trowbridge, Augustus, 62
Truman, Harry S., 195, 196
Trustees, 71, 74
Tschebotarioff, Gregory P., 117, 118
University Hall, 40
Upper Pyne Hall, 79
Vacation, 135
Van Dusen, Henry P., 74, 190
Van Dyke, Henry, 55, 70
Views, see Campus views
Walker Hall, 92
War research projects, 116, 117
Washington, George, 105, 106
Weiman, Elton E., 163
Wertenbaker, Thomas J., 122
West, Andrew F., 62, 72, 73
West College, 30, 31, 34
Wicks, Robert R., 65, 73, 76
Wigner, Eugene P., 116, 188
William III, King, 10
Wilson, Edmund, 145
Wilson, Woodrow, 51, 52, 58, 68, 70, 146, 184
Winans, Samuel R., 60
Witherspoon, John, 4, 106
Witherspoon Hall, 38
World War I, 108-110
World War II, 112-118
Young, Charles A., 28

GPSR Authorized Representative: Easy Access System Europe - Mustamäe tee 50, 10621 Tallinn, Estonia, gpsr.requests@easproject.com

www.ingramcontent.com/pod-product-compliance
Lightning Source LLC
Chambersburg PA
CBHW081419230426
43668CB00016B/2289